I0441994

Skull and Bones

America's Most Powerful and Mysterious Secret Society

Conrad Bauer

Copyrights

All rights reserved. © Conrad Bauer and Maplewood Publishing No part of this publication or the information in it may be quoted from or reproduced in any form by means such as printing, scanning, photocopying, or otherwise without prior written permission of the copyright holder.

Disclaimer and Terms of Use

Effort has been made to ensure that the information in this book is accurate and complete. However, the author and the publisher do not warrant the accuracy of the information, text, and graphics contained within the book due to the rapidly changing nature of science, research, known and unknown facts, and internet. The author and the publisher do not hold any responsibility for errors, omissions, or contrary interpretation of the subject matter herein. This book is presented solely for motivational and informational purposes only. The publisher and author of this book does not control or direct users' actions and are not responsible for the information or content shared, harm and/or action of the book readers. The presentation of the information is without contract or any type of guarantee assurance. This book is not meant to be used, nor should it be used, to diagnose or treat any medical condition. For diagnosis or treatment of any medical problem, consult your own physician. The publisher and author are not responsible for any specific health or allergy needs that may require medical supervision and are not liable for any damages or negative consequences from any treatment, action, application or preparation, to any person reading or following the information in this book. References, if any, are provided for informational purposes only and do not constitute endorsement of any websites or other sources. Readers should be aware that the websites listed in this book, if any, may change.

ISBN: 978-1530910830

Printed in the United States

MAPLEWOOD
— PUBLISHING —

Contents

Introduction

Nobody likes the idea that there are hugely influential powers operating behind closed doors. For centuries, there have been stories about secret societies that control everything we do and dominate the highest echelons of politics and business. Whether it's the Illuminati, the Masons, or the Knights Templar, it's not uncommon for people to believe that there might be a cabal of people who conspire together for their own nefarious purposes. But while these earlier societies might be clouded in mystery and intrigue, there are modern equivalents of which we know much, much more.

One of these mysterious societies is known simply as Skull and Bones. A clandestine group who gather at one of the world's top universities, they are made up of some of the cleverest, brightest, and most privileged members of their generation. In addition to this, their members have gone on to be CEOs, moguls, and even Presidents. Their alumni hold some of the most important positions within society, and for the majority, their membership of this secret club is a closely guarded secret.

Whether it's generations of the Bush family, members of the Taft family, Rockefellers, CIA officers, Presidents, publishers, judges, lawyers, Olympians, ambassadors, congressmen, governors, senators, authors, diplomats, or musicians, there seems no limit on who might be a members. With their suggested involvement in thefts, rituals, and even more hidden power politics, the members of Skull and Bones are part of one of the seemingly most powerful groups in the world. In this book we will examine their history, their practices, their members, and their legacy. By the end, you should have a much clearer idea of what it means to be a member of one of Yale's most exclusive groups: Skull and Bones.

A Brief History of the Order of the Skull and Bones

The history of Skull and Bones might seem simple, but as with many secret societies, attempting to untangle the web of stories, myths, and legends can be incredibly difficult. As such, it is perhaps best to start with a brief overview in which we can examine the commonly accepted narrative, before plunging into greater depth. The theories relating to the history of Skull and Bones are almost as old as the group itself, ensuring that whenever research into the society's history is attempted, one must navigate the murky waters. The society itself has no reason why it should attempt to clarify any part of its history. For them, a murky, confused narrative filled with mistruths simply adds to the aura of the group and distracts from the more truthful elements of what we think we know. By keeping their history conspicuously obscure, Skull and Bones becomes even more of a vague concept. If we want to establish the accepted truth behind the group's history, it can help to turn to an article from Time magazine published in 2009.

As stated in the article in Time magazine, Skull and Bones and its members have been blamed for everything from the Kennedy assassination to the invention of the atomic bomb. The society has been portrayed in negative and positive lights in all sorts of media and has even made an appearance being satirized on the Simpsons. Their involvement in a number of high profile court cases and crimes has bought the group to unexpected levels of attention, prompting a surge in interest. As a response to this, people have tried to assemble as much information as possible on the group. One of the best examples of the group's influence is the election for President of the United States of America that took place in 2004. The election was held between George W. Bush, Republican, and John Kerry, Democrat. As chance would have it, both men were graduates of Yale, and both had been inducted into the secret society. Whichever man ended up taking the White House, America was guaranteed to be overseen by a Bonesman (the name given to the group's members.) Later in this book, we will look into this event in even greater detail.

William Russell

Skull and Bones, as the legends go, was founded by a man named William Russell. Russell, a student at Yale, class of 1833, spent a year in Germany. He found himself wandering between the clandestine and mystical organizations that one might have encountered in 19th Century European high society. These mysterious clubs organized by the elite and the aristocracy would often imitate and replicate legendary organizations such as the Illuminati and the Priory of Scion. Fascinated and enthralled by such a society, Russell took what he had learned from the secretive Germans and brought it back with him to the academic environment of one of America's oldest educational institutions, Yale University. After a supposed falling out between a number of debating societies at the university – Brothers in Unity, the Calliopean Society, and Linonia – who had been arguing about the Phi Beta Kappa ceremony for dishing out the awards, Russell decided that the American institution needed to take the lead from the Germans he had encountered. Teaming with a man named Alphonso Taft, in 1832 the pair founded a group they named as the "Order of the Skull and Bones."

It was not long before the group began to establish its own mythology. The process of inviting someone into the society was in the fashion of similar American university groups. It involved a person being "tapped." This recruitment process was conducted, and with great foresight, Russell managed to foster a spirit of mysterious elitism. Take, for example, the first recruit for the so-called Brotherhood of Death. Alphonso Taft was set to hold an important role in American history, if only for being the father of William H. Taft, the future President of the United States. As the group's first charters indicate, the original name was the "Order of the Scull and Bones," though this common alternative spelling was later corrected.

One of the first legends that was passed down about the activities of the members of Skull and Bones was that they were involved in pagan worship. There were rumors that the group devoted themselves to the goddess Eulogia, an invented creation who was said to represent eloquence. In addition to this, the name was supposed to represent the Order's worship of pirates and other criminals, while they hatched dastardly plans in which world domination was always the end goal. Right from the start, there was an element of the conspiracy theory about what really went on behind the doors of Russell's secret society.

The Russell Trust Association

In recognition of the group's founder, the assets of Skull and Bones are now managed by what is known as the Russell Trust Association. Founded in 1856, the group had been operating for nearly two decades before it was decided that the trust would be required. By this point, the original members had long since graduated, but that did not stop them from taking an active interest. The group ensured that each and every year, a fresh wave of inductees would be tapped, chosen for their reputations on campus and their reputations in the wider world. The Russell Trust Association, founded by both Russell and another Bonesman, Daniel Coit Gilman, was created to ensure that the group's members had a network that existed after their graduation. It would be one in which they could monitor, nurture, and preserve the group from outside the confines of the university system. Gilman himself would prove to be an important man, eventually becoming president of both John Hopkins University and the University of California. He was also one of the founders of the Carnegie Institution. He was perfectly placed to oversee one of the country's most important academic societies.

Looking through the records, one of the first appearances or acknowledgements of the existence of the Skull and Bones outside of their own members can be found in a book by Lyman Bagg. *Four Years at Yale*, published in 1871, tells the story of Bagg's own experiences at the university. While not a member of S&B, and not aware of many of the group's internal machinations, the account demonstrates that in the fifty years following the founding of the group, their reputation and mystery had become part of the Yale folklore. Bagg's book barely mentions Skull and Bones, suggesting instead that the mystery behind the group is a hot bit of gossip among student circles. Though not delving into his own explanations, he notes that many people are fascinated by the group. Without mentioning anything specific, this tells us a number of things about Skull and Bones. First, in just fifty years, their reputation had been cemented among the student body. Second, that the enigmatic qualities of the society were as fascinating then as they are today. Third, Bagg's suggestion that the students "never tire" of dwelling on the group's mysteries tells us that, much like today, a great deal of information regarding Skull and Bones was kept firmly under wraps by all involved. Finally, the lack of background information given by the author indicates the extent to which rumors were commonplace on campus. Bagg never felt the need to go into great detail simply because the amount of speculation that swirled around the society, it seemed, was completely commonplace.

A Yale Society

But why did the group become such a center of attention? There are other groups, societies, and organizations at Yale that offer much of a similar social experience – at least on the surface. Skull and Bones had begun life as a replication of European counterparts, in response to a disagreement among those societies that already existed on campus. The only factors that seemed to differentiate the Order of the Skull and Bones from others were their morbid name, their well-kept secrecy, and the importance and influence of their members. When added together, it seemed as though their very existence was ripe for rumor.

According to Brooks Mather Kelley, the reason behind the interest in Yale's secret societies was simply due to the way in which university life was structured. Due to the recruiting policies of these groups, it was accepted that those who had been at the university a longer amount of time would pass on rumors and stories to the next generation. Like a children's game, these stories might evolve and change as they were being passed around, their features exaggerated for effect or to make the teller seem more knowledgeable or important. With students keen to discover more about life away from their studies, the Order of the Skull and Bones provided them with a mystery that was right on their doorstep, a feature of the very institution they were now a part of. The seniors who then graduated from college, being possessed of more information, would look back over the initiation rituals and the rumors that surrounded such societies and perhaps fuel the fire of salacious stories that spread across campus. In fact, the very nature of Skull and Bones as a secret society meant that they were soon the most talked-about organization on campus. With people desperate to find out more about who they were and what they did, myths and legends began to spring up everywhere. This thought might well have pleased Russell, who intended for his organization to have the same reputation as its European forebears. But more significantly, it meant that – on those times when a morsel of truth did slip into the public domain – it was impossible to separate the truth from the rumor. The lies and stories that grew up around Skull and Bones were their best protection and best recruiting tool. Those who were tapped found themselves keen to learn more, while those who remained on the outside could only guess at what happened within the walls. Accordingly, much of the gossip on campus centered on the Skull and Bones without much real information ever leaving the confines of the Order's own building.

Since these early, mysterious days, Skull and Bones has become known across the country and now the world. Over the centuries, the stories about the group have not just been limited to their role in the university. There have been rumors that they regularly partake in a ritual whereupon they steal the skulls of famous people. Perhaps the most notorious of these is the skull of Native American leader Geronimo, whose missing cranium has been the subject of much speculation. This practice – known as "crooking" – will be covered later in the book, but it seems like one of the many theories that make up a tapestry of rumors surrounding the Order. Over time, the persistence of such stories has meant that the practice is now part of Skull and Bones law.

In a similar manner, the lack of concrete information about the Order has led many people to try to fill in the gaps themselves. The Internet has become one of the greatest tools in the world for uncovering information about previously hidden matters. One need only look at the leaks of government material by Edward Snowden or organizations such as WikiLeaks to see that there is a means of distributing information about the previously clandestine. But along with the massive resources that we now have at our disposal, there is also a more debilitating side to the Internet that can hinder investigations. It can be tough to uncover correct and legitimate findings when so many websites are content to post unproven and speculative pieces regarding organizations such as Skull and Bones. Often, these conspiracy websites will be happy to distribute unverified and often untrue information simply to further theories and agendas. Information such as this must be separated and quarantined when conducting investigations into real-life matters. In truth, the emergence of the Internet has meant that the Order's collegiate reputation has grown. Just as rumors and misinformation spread across a 19th Century College campus adding to the notorious legend of the Order, the details that are circulated on the Internet fulfil much the same purpose. In this regard, trying to learn about the Order of Skull and Bones is just as difficult now as it was one hundred years ago.

Fact and Fiction

So then, that leaves us with one particularly tricky question: if we are to examine the history of the Order of the Skull and Bones, how can we separate fact from fiction? One of the best and most popular ways is to rely on the accounts given by the members themselves. If there is anything in which we can put greater amounts of trust regarding the Order, it is their members. The membership list of the group is one of the worst-kept secrets around. This is based on a number of reasons. First, no members really make any effort to hide their involvement from the public eye. As mentioned previously, a number of Bonesmen have held the highest office in American politics. While we know that Presidents have been members and have admitted to being involved, they very rarely actually discuss what happened within the confines of the Order.

Second, the involvement of people within societies on the Yale campus is often public knowledge. As well as the 19th Century societies we have already mentioned, there are a number of organizations that have sprung up in the wake of Skull and Bones replicating their secret stylings. Wolf's Head, the Scroll and Key, Book and Snake, and Berzelius have all risen at some point during the Order's history. One of the chief concerns shared among these groups is keeping information on who is involved in which society. It's been well known that the societies keep tabs on one another's members, often documenting in a charter or log book just who belongs to which society. Once a prospect is tapped, they can begin a long journey during which they are often observed at every step.

Finally, one of the most obvious reasons as to why the membership of the Order of the Skull and Bones is not too secret is simply because it is common knowledge which buildings they own. For years, the society has used many of the same meeting halls and congregation points. It would take an interested party arriving at these locations in any given year to write down who arrives at the door and who is allowed admittance. Added to this, thanks to the Russell Trust Association, we can look into the properties owned by the group and learn about those involved by following the paper trial.

As such, we can take it for granted that the membership itself into the group is not hidden. This is why so many histories of the Skull and Bones organization depend upon the membership lists for their starting point and seek to extrapolate information from there. However, this can be a dangerous practice and – as we will see later in this book – the actual details of the history of the members is far more interesting than people realize. There is a strict selection criteria that must be observed when the Order is tapping new recruits, and it is these people who form the bulk of the members.

A Fascinating Society

So then, if the information about who is able to join this secret society is so public, what makes the membership of the Order of the Skull and Bones so fascinating? Put simply, it is the information that we do not know which is typically the most tantalizing. There have been rumors, hints, and admissions about the variety of practices that are involved in the group. Tales of the occult, of strange initiation rituals, of extreme financial power, and influence beyond the grave have pervaded the legacy of the Order. Involvement in the group by so many powerful people over the years is, quite simply, not a coincidence. Instead, trying to determine what it is about the Order that imbues its members with such power, wealth, and influence becomes the chief point of interest for many people. As we look through the strict rules of the Order, their exploits, and the stories from their ex-members, and the conspiracies that surround them, we will begin to see just what it is that makes the prospect of the Skull and Bones such as thrilling proposition for so many people. As we break further from the known history of the group and delve deeper into the muddy waters, you might well be shocked and appalled by what we discover within. Now that we've given a brief outline of the group's existence, it's time to uncover more about the Order of the Skull and Bones.

Buildings, Branding, and Borrowed Signs

It might seem strange to some that a university society should own and operate a number of buildings and facilities. While the majority of organizations that gather in academic buildings can rely upon renting the odd hall or room or choose to meet in public places, the means by which Skull and Bones is able to make use of their own facilities is slightly different. They are not a fraternity, nor do they offer living quarters to those who become members. Instead, the buildings that are under their realm of influence are typically used once or twice a week, usually for a few hours. It might seem odd then, that such a group should own and operate a number of premises purely for the purpose of conducting their secret meetings. But when you realize the depth of wealth that is available to the former Bonesmen, as well as the close connections many alumni bear to the society, it should come as no surprise to see that so many people are willing to fund the facilities that allow the Order of the Skull and Bones to function in continued secrecy.

Yale

In order to get the best perspective on the history of the Order's use of buildings on campus, it is important to journey back through the history of societies on the Yale campus and understand the precedents that dictated how and when Russell's Order would meet. For the best example, we should look at Phi Beta Kappa, a chapter of which formed at Yale in 1780. Loosely standing (in Latin) for Philosophia Biou Kybernetes (or Love of Wisdom, the Guide of Life), the group sought to promote and endorse literature and friendly interchanges between the scholars at Yale, meeting and discussing topics such as politics, philosophy, ethics, and religion. There were other, similar groups at Yale from these times, including the Brothers in Unity and Linonia, centuries-old societies that focused on scholarly issues. Unlike these two groups, however, Phi Beta Kappa (or PBK) was designed to keep its activities a secret. For those on the outside, the membership of PBK and the occurrences within the confines of the society were a mystery. With a membership composed of supposedly the best students at the university (plus a number of their less scholarly associates who were allowed in by merits of their acquaintances), the secret group was the forebear of the secret societies that would come later. They seemed to have the endorsement of the establishment, to the extent that they knew which members to recruit thanks to information gathered from the faculty.

The meeting practices of PBK formed the foundation for later secret societies at the university. Meetings were regular but not too often. At first, the group met once every two weeks, though this was eventually reduced to once a month. Their choice of location for these meetings was a building that was known to belong to another strange organization, the Freemasons. For anyone who has done their research into secret societies around the world, the Freemasons are a group whose name appears often and in many places. Loosely thought to be a social endeavor with knowledge and involvement ramping up as one moves higher through the ranks of the Order, many important people and many unimportant people have had some degree of involvement with the Freemasons. That one of Yale's first secret societies should share their meeting hall speaks of a close connection between the two and establishes a precedent of intimate knowledge that will echo along the annals of the university's history.

These sessions, meeting in the Freemasons hall, were scheduled for 6:30pm and would start on the dot. At each, there was typically a speech given by one of the members, and then a debate was held in which some of the most pressing matters of ethics or philosophy were bandied back and forth. For members who arrived late, there was a fine of sixpence, while those PBK members who skipped the meeting entirely were fined ten dollars, a not inconsequential sum at the time. That there should be a ten dollar fine tells of the importance of the meetings and of the resources of the members. For those members who were considered to have "flunked an appointment," the fine was doubled to twenty dollars. Once a year, around Christmas time, there would be a large dinner held for the PBK members. At these dinners, a graduated former member would deliver a speech, and then the officers for the next year would be elected. From what we know of what happened during these meetings, the PBK organization was not involved in a great deal of mysterious activity. What drove the intrigue into the organization derived simply from their insistence on secrecy. Those who found themselves on the outside of the PBK circle were desperate to know what their fellow students were doing. This escalated to the point, when in 1786, three senior students knocked down the door of the secretary of the PBK and stole the society's secret papers that had been hidden in a trunk. It is not known what they uncovered, as a team of PBK members tracked down the guilty parties and sat them before a PBK council. In front of the council, the three seniors were compelled to sign written confessions – purely voluntary, of course – in which they promised never to tell anyone what they had learned from the papers (if there had even been anything at all.) The intrigue surrounding the event escalated even further, to the point where the trunk was stolen again just a year and half later.

A Need for Secrecy

But secrecy among Yale societies would become a bone of contention, not just among the students, but among the United States as a whole. It's possible to look at the events surrounding PBK in the 1830s to see just how suspicious people were becoming of the Masons and their influence, with the PBK on the Yale campus becoming a microcosm of this attitude. The first hints of rebellion came in 1830, when something called the Great Conic Sections Rebellion took place. Yale of the 19th Century was very different to that of today. One of the requisites for a Yale education was the ability to recite what was known as the conic sections. These were mathematical formulae and figures relating to the geometric curves that might be found in circles and ellipses. As part of their education, Yale students were expected to be able to recite these conic sections and were tested accordingly. Fury was sparked when some students accused their more privileged counterparts of being allowed to depend on books and resources during the test. They wanted the same opportunity. When faced with their examinations, they steadfastly refused to listen to the faculty.

The university was furious. They took action against the students, claiming that they had formed a "combination to resist the government." After this, all Yale classes were suspended and students were forced to sign a document that ensured that they agreed to obey the rules and laws of the institution. Nearly half of the 1832 class refused to sign and were forcibly expelled from Yale. Their names were placed on a blacklist, and they were never allowed to attend another university. These events occurred against the backdrop of a widespread anti-masonic movement in the United States. People were beginning to grow distrustful of the extent to which this secret society could influence the government. A presidential candidate emerged with the promise of dispelling America's secret societies, echoing the same resentment of privilege that had compelled the Yale students to stand up. At the university, this growing distrust of secret societies meant that PBK was forced to abandon their more secretive policies. Already the most suspected group on campus, their fondness for clandestine meetings in Freemason halls meant that they were at the center of the masonic scandal running through America.

As a response, many of PBK's secrets were published. The secret handshakes they used and the signs they had invented were made public knowledge. All of their secret ceremonies were banned. Soon it seemed that as the secrecy was stripped from PBK, they lost their allure. Without the secrecy that had intrigued so many, few people were that interested in another, run-of-the-mill Yale society. PBK lost many of its members to the scandal and eventually closed their doors for many decades. The Order of the Skull and Bones was founded in the aftermath of the PBK scandal. As Phi Beta Kappa diminished in popularity, a far more secretive and clandestine group took their place. They learned lessons from PBK, and it seems that one of the key factors that Russell incorporated into the establishing of the Order was the need for their own private quarters, one which would not associate them with the Freemasons and tar them with the same brush that had led to the downfall of one of Yale's premier secret organizations.

Russell's Version

In fact, the emergence of Russell's group bears closer bonds to the fall of PBK than you might expect. It was in the academic year of 1832 to 1833 that a man named William Russell, the valedictorian of the 1833 class, was elected secretary of the Yale PBK chapter. As secretary, he was included in the process of electing the next wave of PBK officers and was shocked to discover that one of those he felt best suited to the positions – Eleazar Kingsbury Foster – had been purposefully left of the election slate. Apoplectic, he came out and openly condemned the PBK, and by December of 1832, had colluded with Foster to recruit 13 other students, among them Alfonso Taft, to take what they had learned from the PBK downfall and begin a brand new secret society, the Order of the Skull and Bones. Russell had been an elected secretary of Phi Beta Kappa. Few knew better how the organization was run and how it related to the Yale establishment. It is clear that Russell learned the essentials of the American secret academic society and combined it with his knowledge of the European models that he had been exposed to. Thanks to the anti-masonic scandal, Russell knew that the meeting of the upper-echelons of the student body must be more secret than ever before. As such, the need for secrecy in Skull and Bones was paramount. While PBK had used their mysterious operations to build up a reputation, Skull and Bones were forced to be secret if they wanted to continue to meet. Had they been discovered, they would have been expelled and blacklisted.

The combination of European and American models of the secret society can be seen in the way in which Skull and Bones first began to brand themselves. It is thought that the obsession with death- and bone-orientated imagery is a reflection of an unnamed society that Russell discovered when touring through Germany. He brought back this morbid branding, combined it with the structural organization and practices of his PBK experiences, and began to build a secret society that fused together the best of both continents. There is some evidence to suggest that Skull and Bones is, in fact, just another chapter in just another, much older organization. Documents have been discovered from within the halls which seem to suggest there were jubilee and anniversary celebrations of the establishing of an "American chapter." Another document, taken from 1933, celebrates the anniversary of the society's "Yale chapter." When considering these theories, there is a huge lack of evidence, chiefly the name of the parent organization. Skull and Bones contains many features and practices that are somewhat unique to the American interpretation of a secret society. However, it is likely that William Russell wished to lend credence to his nascent organization by tying its history together with more celebrated predecessors. Rather than a chapter, it could well be the spiritual continuity of the older European models that are so celebrated by the group. Rather than attempting to trace the group's history back to the ancient orders in Europe – which is slightly disingenuous – we can instead recognize the emergence of the Order of the Skull and Bones as the establishment of a brand new superpower among American secret societies. In order to build their foundations of credibility, Russell borrowed heavily from the European influence, likely wished to suggest a common heritage with many of these groups, and nowhere is this more evident than in the buildings themselves.

The Tomb

Ask anyone about buildings belonging to the Order of Skull and Bones and the most common response will be about the Tomb. A morbid name, it certainly ties in with the ideas of death that surrounded so much of the group's branding and symbolism. However, the Tomb, while being the most notorious home of the Order, was only built some two decades after the founding of the organization. Construction of the first wing of the building began in 1856, while additional sections were added later. In 1903, for example, a second wing was added onto the structure, while a set of Neo-Gothic towers were erected in the garden in the rear of the building in 1912.

The architectural decisions hearken back to Europe and the Old World, using an Egypto-Doric blend that calls to mind Greek architecture. Suitable for a society established on the basis of ancient philosophy and ethics, the columns at the rear are both a throwback to this European heritage and help form an enclosed space around the rear of the building. To look at it, the Tomb is both intimidating and almost unremarkable. There is very little of note, which is in itself noteworthy. Designed to be both inconspicuous and imposing at the same time, it offers no answers about what happens inside and provide little other than clues as to its intended purpose. Many of the architects involved with the developing building have either been Bonesmen themselves or have been related to members. Accordingly, every addition is a carefully considered extension of the group's ideology.

When stepping inside, the link to Europe's secret societies is apparent. Not much has changed in the years since the Tomb was first constructed and decorated, and many of the accounts we have of its interior remain consistent to this day. A number of German artifacts – coats of arms, artworks – can be found hanging from the walls, while there is a repeated use of German-language mottos written across the walls. One picture, as described by a witness, features a number of imagery-heavy additions. The composition is of a burial vault left deliberately open. Around the vault are four human skulls, arranged on the stone slab to surround a jester's hat. There is also a book left open, a number of mathematical instruments, a beggar's cup, and an abandoned crown. Written in German is a riddle. The riddle asks the audience which man was the wise one and which one the fool, asking them to choose between the beggar and the king. Finally, inscribed beneath – again in German – is a motto proclaiming that both the rich and the poor are equal in death. The picture is a fine example of the aesthetic form within the Tomb and the eye is drawn to a small card positioned next to the picture, which says that the painting was a gift from the Order's "German chapter."

Elsewhere on the walls are five photographs of typical scenes from the day-to-day life of German students. The photographs are clearly quite old, though the legend bears no indication as to whom they might be portraying or which German society they depict. It's not just pictures that represent the adoption of German student culture throughout the halls of the Tomb. If you happen to arrive on one of the busier nights in the social calendar, you might well hear the refrains of the members as they sing a selection of the Skull and Bones songs that have been conjured especially for the society. Though most are unknown, it has been confirmed by at least one source that the original tune for one of the hymns is "Deutschland Uber Alles," a famed German anthem written by the composer Haydn. Experts on the society's history have made a point to separate the pars of the organization from the present. There was a time, they point out, when the society owed a great debt to the existence of its European equivalents and strove to replicate itself after their customs and aesthetics. Though many of the aesthetics still remain, they are largely decorative now, and any channels of communication that might have existed between Skull and Bones and German societies is now restricted or at least kept a secret to the majority of members. Instead, the influence and power of the modern members is enough to elevate Skull and Bones to one of the most important organizations worldwide. While Germany might have been a leading world superpower in the 19th Century, there is no doubt that today the United States occupies that position.

The Traditions

This changing adherence to traditions might strike some as odd. For many, the expected behavior of a secret society is that it would demand absolute knowledge of the society's past by its members and a reverence for what has come before. But the Order of Skull and Bones is different. For an excellent example of why this is the case, we need only turn to a pamphlet produced in 1933 and given to new members. Produced on the centenary of the group's founding and designed to provide a "continuation of the history of our order," the pamphlet declares quite emphatically that there is "no History of the Bones." Phrased as a confession on behalf of the reader, those who are exposed to the pamphlet are compelled to agree that there is nothing else but the Order itself. Rather than having a set of traditions, it states that the "heavy thinkers of the barbarian 20th century" might be perplexed by such problems, but true Bonesmen know that there is nothing of worth other than the Order, and as such, the history of the European ties and the founding of Skull and Bones is simply an afterthought. What is important is the present and how it can affect the current members.

At first, however, the Tomb was not available to the members of the Order of the Skull and Bones. During the early days, there was still a sense of danger and secrecy that demanded the group hide themselves from the Yale authorities. As such, they started with an unassuming name. Titled the Eulogian Club, the group could seem to pass for any other generic society or even church organization should the authorities even investigate further. Still keeping itself from the public eye, the bland name acted as a shield against prying eyes and offered members the chance to pass off their whereabouts and actions without implicating other Bonesmen. At first, many of the recruits were picked from members of a more traditional society, those who Russell and his friends felt fit the template. Together, they began to gather in meetings, and the Order of the Skull and Bones began to take on a more familiar aesthetic. It was a year before the sign of the Skull and Bones began to appear around campus. The group would often meet in a chapel, far away from the Freemason hall that might raise suspicion.

The first record of any sort of recognition from the faculty towards the new society came in 1833. As far as we can tell, the Yale authorities were alerted to a meeting that had gotten particularly out of hand. They called an emergency meeting on Christmas Day to look into the group. After a short discussion, it was decided that nine members of the new society would receive letters warning them to cease their actions and another letter would be sent to their parents. Among those who received the letters were the future treasurer of Yale, a man who would become a congressman, and a person destined to sit on the Supreme Court of Louisiana. After the letters were sent out, the group pulled back further from public view and began to guard their actions with greater efficiency.

Another important piece of Skull and Bones branding would arrive shortly after. Along with the name – as well as the cover name, the Eulogian Club, supposedly in reference to the invented god of eloquence – there was a marked increase in the use of a specific number. Early on in the society's life, the number "322" begins to appear more and more frequently. There have been many theories as to why this exact number was chosen. Some have suggested that it might tie into numerology or the ancient Jewish mysticism, Kabbalah. Other people have pointed out that the renowned Greek philosopher Demosthenes died in the year 322 BC. There have been suggestions in the laws and histories of the Skull and Bones that the year 322 BC is given as the day on which Eulogia (their invented goddess) ascended up unto heaven, set to return in the year 1832 with the founding of the society. This is certainly the cover story given for the use of the number 322, which is used by every member when signing official, relevant documents. When communicating with another Bonesman, for example, it is common to see the phrase "yours in 322" appear alongside the signatures. However, the story is only given certain amounts of credence among some scholars, who suspect that it is simply a convenient explanation for something more complex and potentially controversial. Until we are able to uncover more specific information, we can only report the theories. With the explanation likely being one of the most closely guarded secrets, however, this particular piece of Bones lore and branding will remain a mystery for the foreseeable future.

While we might not know the reason for the repeated use of 322 among the Bonesmen, our investigations note that it is not something that is forgotten upon leaving Yale. One of the most commonly cited examples is the donation that was made to the society anonymously when George W. Bush became a member in 1967, with a check issued to the tune of $322,000. Another example is the office extension number of a man named David Thorne. Thorne is not only the former brother-in-law of John Kerry (a Bonesman), but was his campaign manager and friend, himself a member of the Order during the 1960s. Thorne, when selecting the extension number for his office phone, personally requested number 322.

A Legitimate Branch

Things changed slightly in 1856, when the Russell Trust Association became an actual extension of the society. Following this move, the Order could stop their scattered meetings across campus. Nearly two decades after the original founding of the group, there were now enough alumni to gather together the funds for a permanent home. Inside, the Bonesmen could decorate and detail in their idiosyncratic manner. Rather than having to move constantly around campus, hanging up Skull and Bones signs and leaving their 322 mark wherever they met, the Russell Trust Association meant that they could meet up and conduct their business away from prying eyes. Following the persecution of secret societies during the early days, the furor had died down and once again there was a place on the Yale campus for a secret society who wanted to gather together the very best the university had to offer but away from the constant gaze attached to many, more mainstream groups.

At the time of construction, the Tomb cost the Order between $7,000 and $8,000. This was not an inconsequential sum for the time and speaks of the amount of investment and resources that were at the disposal of those who had an active interest in the group. According to the documents we have been able to recover, $5,300 was designated for the wall, foundations, and the structure of the building, while the remainder was spent on furnishing the property. The brown sandstone walls give nothing away to the casual observer, creating a depth of color that seems to draw in anything of interest without revealing anything about the contents of the building. Similarly, the dark glass used means that the windows allow in only a small amount of light and prevent those on the outside from catching a glimpse of what might happen on the inside. Of course, with the property designed to host functions and celebrations, there must be a kitchen and servants' quarters. These are contained in the depths of the building and are found near the heavy iron emergency exit. All around the building, as is typical for New Haven, there are thin, spindly trees. During the long winter months, these bare trunks look like the bones which lend the society its morbid name.

In all, the Tomb is three stories high, with an attic space located at the top of the building. While the construction work itself has interested many who have attempted to read secrets into the design decisions that have been made through the ages, often the best way in which to get an insight into the ethos of the society is to consider the number of possessions that line the walls. As we will discover later in the book, the way in which the Order chose to decorate the property (and in particular, the items they acquired) holds great sway in how they present themselves. There are examples of ancient taxidermy, flickering candles, suited knights in ancient armor, flags from boats and ships, traditional blankets from around the world hidden inside old trunks, tributes to Buddha who rides atop an elephant, and – with another link to 322 BC – statues of Demosthenes. These items have been accumulated throughout the society's long history, each one speaking to one aspect of the group's mysterious ideology. The overall effect, however, is eerily intimidating. The sheer volume of paraphernalia can overwhelm, while the low lighting and morbid quality of many pieces can put many people on edge.

The large majority of these items are gifts from former members. As well as these curiosities, a common donation from ex-members are pieces of art. Over the time in which the Order has been active, they have received a number of paintings from their alumni, all fitting a similar theme. Those most befitting of the Skull and Bones moniker are pieces such as the one donated by Russell Cheney, an oil painting of dancing skeletons gathered in a garden. The majority of the modern decoration was handled by John Walter Cross, an architect who was part of the Order during the turn of the 19th Century. The skeletal figures are common and skulls litter many nooks and crannies. Elsewhere in the house, donations such as the complete works of Demosthenes and a first edition of the experimental novel *The Life and Opinons of Tristram Shandy* demonstrate the importance of considered literature and philosophy. It might seem, when entering the Tomb, that there one is entering a Victorian menagerie. But in truth, each item is considered and chosen for the effect it imparts on the unassuming observer.

American University Life

But, as we have mentioned, there is always an indication within the Skull and Bones that it is an American society. Nothing says this better than the tribute to America's game, baseball. A fitting tribute to the Order's loyalty to their academic institute can be found stored in a glass case in a distant corner of the building. Behind this glass are a number of gilded baseballs, each taken from games involving the Yale team. Written nearby are the dates and names of the games in which they were used, remembering the university's history, commemorating the country's most popular sport, and demonstrating the wealth and importance of the society in one fell swoop.

There have been recent reports from certain modern members that the interior of the Tomb is not quite as grand as it might once have been. Though the Order is still an important and wealthy society on campus, the sheer amount of donated items and gifts they have received has meant that the inside has become crowded, and certain items have been difficult to maintain. Still used as much as it ever was, the Tomb suffers from being a strange combination of museum, political statement, and functioning society hall all at once.

As you might expect from a society named Skull and Bones, there is a consistent emphasis on death. War and its tumultuous effects are a constant theme, with many of the Bonesmen being involved in conflicts at home and abroad. Everything from Civil War rifles to the boots from World War II serve to remind the members of the constancy of death, as well as German helmets and machine guns that are found along various passageways. A little hint at the morbid humor can be found in one Latin inscription, "tempus fugit," which translates as "time flies." Added to this, there are skeletons, skulls, and bones of both humans and animals. The crockery, the cutlery, and the painted panels on the wall are all emblazoned with the group's familiar skull imagery, while cups and mugs are fashioned in the shape of skulls. Throughout the entire building, death is not only presented as a threatening image, but it is also celebrated and cherished. This is exemplified by the tablet laid down in the main foyer that bears a dedication to "the departed Bones," warning the living that they should remember that "you must die."

When discussing why the Order of the Skull and Bones is seemingly obsessed with death, a former member of the society suggested that it was a deliberate decision to remind the current members of their place within the world. The purpose of the décor is to offer up a self-aggrandizing message to those who are walking the halls. Despite the large amount of power and influence that many Bonesmen already (and/or will eventually) wield, they should remember that are at the mercy of mortality as much as the next man. The skull of a king, members are constantly reminded, looks just like that of a pauper. While this message might be popular among the Bonesmen and something the society holds aloft, it certainly is increasing the attention that the group receives from elsewhere. Indeed, the imagery of the Order of the Skull and Bones society is certainly eye-catching and leads many people to believe that there's an ulterior, sinister motive to all of their actions.

The Inner Temple

At the center of the Tomb, however, there is one room that is a little bit different. Named the Inner Temple, or simply Room 322, it is the most private part of the property and the place where the most secret of rituals take place. Getting in is difficult. The door is huge, a locked and bolted iron slab that has held firm against a number of break-ins that have taken place over the years. The room inside is a rough square, with each side measuring close to fourteen feet. Wainscoting rises up the first four feet of the walls above which are hung the most cherished oil paintings in the building. Other than the door, the only other interruption is the black marble fireplace. As you step in, you immediately cross over a mosaic that depicts, once again, the number 322. Look up and you'll see an engraving on the far wall, with the number again emblazoned, this time beneath the name Demosthenes. Skull and Bones imagery is everywhere in the minutest of details. The roof is something unexpected, however, opening up to a sky blue dome with a small skylight placed right in the center. The light shines down onto a table that is permanently set up in the room, which holds the same items every single day: a skull balanced carefully on a cushion, and an hourglass filled with sand that will measure out exactly five minutes.

This is the room where a number of strange rituals and ceremonies are performed. These will be covered later in the book, though it can be important to note that there is a small tocsin (the type of bell one might normally find in a church) that is rung during these occasions. There are rumors that this is the same bell that belonged to Yale University during its early years, which was sounded to signify events on campus. There is also a large grandfather clock of unknown origin, made identifiable by the skull and crossbones written across its face. Situated beneath an ancient Yale flag, the clock has been featured in photos we have of members posing inside the society walls. Scattered across the room are further items of significance to the organization, whether they are skulls or a pair of spectacles that are rumored to belong to a former president of the university.

The feature of the Inner Temple that most catches the eye, however, is the looming specter of a large case, within which is placed a human skeleton. Known among the Bonesmen as "the Madame," due to the fact that many believed the bones to belong to Madame de Pompadour (a mistress of the French King Louis XV.) Sections of the case to the sides of the skeleton hold some of the Order's most valuable and treasured possessions, while a child-sized coffin is placed at the feet of the Madame. The coffin's former occupant, suitably smaller, can be found hanged just above the mantelpiece. Beneath the child skeleton is a small gilded frame that features a small gold door. Reaching behind this will reveal a small switch, that when pressed, opens a secret compartment, in which is hidden a wooden engraving of the goddess Eulogia.

In order to gain access to the Inner Temple, one will need to procure the skeleton key. This is hidden away in a separate room named the Nest. Aside from the Nest and the Inner Temple, the other most secure place in the building is found in the northwest part of the Tomb. There is a single wooden step that leads up to a walk-in vault, decorated in black. To get in, one must know the combination lock that is changed on a regular basis. The contents are not public knowledge, but it has been theorized that this is the place where the society keeps their most important pieces. This could be information about the members, details of their finances, information they have regarding other societies on campus or around the world, data gathered about the faculty and the rest of Yale, and anything else they deem too valuable to risk exposing to those who gain entry to the main building. As well as this, the room next to the vault is a striking contrast. Just as the reminders of the mortality of both rich and poor are spread through the building, the most valuable items are kept next to what seems to be a junk room. Whereas the vault contains the most important items, right next door is the storage room for anything not deemed worthy of being put out in the house, including rumors of broken skulls and even a fake head of a gorilla. Though the contrast might seem striking, there are one or two people who claim that this apparent junk room is simply another disguise, and that some of the most valuable items are hidden among the junk, secreted away in plain view.

Other Locations

But the Tomb is not the only place that Skull and Bones has used to house its affairs. There may be many properties that come under the banner of the Russell Trust Association or various shell companies, but the only other place we can be sure that it has used in the past is much more secluded than their regular meeting places. Found in the middle of the St. Lawrence River, Deer Island is a retreat owned and operated by the Order of the Skull and Bones. Covering close to forty acres, it has been closely detailed by many people who have somehow gained access to the island. Intended to offer somewhere quiet where Bonesmen can gather together and rekindle their friendships, it has seen a great deal of development over the years, though less attention has been paid to it recently.

Around a century ago, Deer Island featured many of the luxurious trappings of the rich and powerful. There were supposedly a number of tennis courts and even a softball field. The surrounding plant life includes gooseberry bushes and rhubarb, though those in search of a real meal are catered to by the servants and chefs who arrive by the catboats situated all over the river. It was common for elegant and ostentatious dinner parties and gatherings to be held on the island, which is far from the public view and the prying eyes of the university authorities. It is tradition that each and every new recruit into the Order must visit the island at one point or another, though it is commonly accepted that the location has fallen into a state of disrepair as the society has lost interest in using it as a retreat. Whether this means that they now go elsewhere or whether there is genuinely no need for such a location, it is still owned by the Russell Trust Association and will continue to be regarded as one of the Bonesmen's most important sites. There have even been reports of fires on the island, which seems to imply burned out houses and abandoned buildings, having been described as being "basically ruins" these days.

It seems as though Deer Island was more geared towards the legacy aspects of the Skull and Bones experience. While the Tomb was the designated gathering point for those who were still attending Yale, it would not suffice for welcoming home those who had graduated and wished to reminisce over their university days. Due to the high profile of many of their alumni, the secrecy offered by Deer Island in the 19th and early 20th Centuries meant that the rich and powerful could arrive there to meet without having their privacy compromised. But in this age of telephoto lenses and drone aircraft, Deer Island does not offer the same promise of isolation that it once did. Couple that with the fact that it is now one of the best-known parts of the Skull and Bones mythos, it should be no surprise to see that the island has fallen out of favor as a meeting place.

Instead, the best place for Bonesmen who require a bit of privacy might well be back on the campus of Yale University. While it might seem counterintuitive to think that the most hidden of places is the one so closely associated with the Order, there is more to their property than meets the eye. It is commonly accepted that the Tomb has at least one secret tunnel. Though there may be more, the only one which has been confirmed offers Bonesmen a direct route from the Tomb to a tiny hidden garden. The tunnel itself it lit by candle light and painted in a blood-red hue. A winding spiral staircase leads travelers through the gloom and towards the gothic towers. From here, the Bonesmen can survey the entire campus (jokingly referred to as "the realm," tellingly) and can hide from those who might be keeping the front entrance under close guard. Between the two towers is an enclosed courtyard that resembles something from a medieval monastery. Featuring a mosaic, a patio, a set of sculptures, and a bench, it was constructed in 1872 by Theodore Woolsey and intended to offer solitude and quiet to society members. Capable of fitting around fifteen people, it is perfect for those most private of gatherings that must be kept under wraps at all costs. With hidden spaces such as these, and the ongoing penchant for morbid branding, it should not be a surprise to learn that so many people tie the Order of the Skull and Bones to nefarious purposes.

Rites, Rituals, and Initiation

Think about any campus-based society or fraternity, and one of the most common questions always involves the initiation ceremony. Whether it's a simple oath, a harsh hazing, or something decidedly more sinister, the ways in which people are inducted into university societies holds a huge amount of interest to those who have not passed through the process. For people who are on the outside looking in, the induction into any kind of society seems like it would involve a bizarre and complicated ceremony that makes little sense. When we combine this with the similar practices in the Freemasons and other secret societies, it is expected that the Order of the Skull and Bones must possess some ritualistic means of initiating their members into the group. As such, the rites, rituals, and initiation ceremony of the Order is one of the most hotly contested and fascinating parts of studying the group.

Rituals and Rumors

One of the main reasons why people obsess over the various initiation processes that are used in campus societies is the way in which the media has portrayed them. Likely based on some truth, mixed with interpretation and exaggeration, everyone expects these ceremonies to be humiliating, strange, and tinged with something of the occult. Often, it is thought, the ritual will be so embarrassing or demeaning as to bond the inductee to the group for the rest of time. Should these details get out, it is suggested, then their reputation will be left in ruin. Put simply, those who are searching for these kind of rites and initiations are often left wanting. But in an Order where there is already a heavy obsession with the morbid, the close proximity of many occult items, and a reputation for involving some of the most powerful people to have come out of Yale in the last century and a half, the means of entering into the Order of the Skull and Bones is certainly strange.

Like every property owned by a society on the Yale campus, there is an acknowledgement that only society members should be allowed inside. While other organizations might be lax with these rules and may allow for guests and invited parties, the Skull and Bones society keep their priorities strict. Walking in to the Tomb, one of the first things that one might see is an old sign from a dusty backwater part of Middle America. While the sign is likely stolen, the words echo true with the sentiment expressed by every single Bonesman around. "This is a private club," the sign states in capital letters, "be prepared to show membership card." The sign, however, is something of a side joke. To gain entrance to the Temple, one must need much more than just a card.

Rosenbaum

Interest in the Order of the Skull and Bones is not new. In 2001, for example, the investigative journalist Ron Rosenbaum began to grow more and more interested in the rumours of the activities that were happening within the walls of the Tomb and the influence which Skull and

Bones was beginning to have on the world of American politics. In all, Rosenbaum has spent close to twenty-five years investigating secret societies and was able to uncover what he believed to be the very first account of what one of the Order's initiation ceremonies looks like. Acquiring an audiotape of the ceremony supposed to have taken place in 2000, he came across the recording after being approached by a student. Building on this, Rosenbaum professed to have infiltrated the group and used night vision recording equipment to glance into the ground of the Tomb in 2001. Able to record both audio and video, they were supposedly able to look into the courtyard that the Bonesmen believed to be their secluded sanctuary. According to the journalist, the recording that was made depicts a man representing the former Bonesman and then-recently elected President George W. Bush. He was locked in a heated debate with an unnamed person, in which he threatened to "ream" the other party just as he had "reamed Al Gore" (who had been Bush's opponent in the Presidential race).

According to Rosenbaum, this was all part of the ceremony. Rather than part of a high stakes political battle, these arguments came down to screamed threats thrown by the Bonesmen towards those who were hoping to join the Order. Along with the aforementioned comments, there were references to Abner Louima, a Haitian immigrant who had recently made the news after being tortured by the NYPD. There was shouting and screaming, with demands such as "lick my bum-hole, neophyte" being flung towards the potential recruits. The ceremony closed when one of the authoritative figures broke out a butcher's knife. Wearing nothing but animal furs, he wielded the blade in front of the recruits, standing over a nude woman who seemed to be covered in blood. The so-called "neophyte" was then forced to approach a skull placed just a few feet from the body and lean down to kiss it on the polished bone. As his lips met the skull, the man with the knife bent down and carefully rubbed the blade along the neophyte's neck, pretending to slit his throat. With that, the recording ends and the figures move back into the building.

Rosenbaum has since used this footage to put forward a number of theories about what took place that night. According to the journalist, this ceremony was evidence of the extent to which the group has exerted control over media moguls, diplomats, spies, and bankers. Rituals such as this can be used, he says, to seal their involvement in a lifelong fraternity and brotherhood, supplying the group with direct access to huge amounts of power. But while these accusations have often been levelled at Skull and Bones (simply due to the demographics of their alumni), Rosenbaum's accusations went further. He suggested that the CIA might be involved, as well as Time Inc., a Secretary of State, and a group of National Security Advisors under the Order's control. He goes on to say that events such as the bombing of Hiroshima and Nagasaki, the invasion of the Bay of Pigs, and the Vietnam war were all inventions of the families who had passed through the annals of the Order of the Skull and Bones, such as the Tafts, the Bundys, and the Lovetts. According to him, they all took part in the ritual his film depicted and were thus bonded to the society for life.

The release of the footage cause quite a shock. It even got mentioned in mainstream media, such as ABC News, who ran images and clips from the footage and interviewed Rosenbaum about what he had seen and what he belied it meant. It was described as a "great day" in the history of American investigative journalism by some sneering commentators, who didn't quite believe that Rosenbaum deserved the attention that he so clearly adored. But it was a worldwide sensation. As far away as Sweden, people were discussing the Skull and Bones initiation ceremony. It further cemented the idea of the Order as an international force to be reckoned with and made Rosenbaum's name, however briefly, famous around the world. It speaks of just how suspicious people are of the Order and their reputation that people were so willing to belief the story.

An Alternate Story

However, there have been aspersions cast over the veracity of Rosenbaum's footage. One graduate of Yale (and a member of other societies) described the ritual as being "too vulgar" for the Order of the Skull and Bones. Rather than a display of obvious power and imagery, this person was under the impression that the ceremony for initiating the new members of the organization was rather a process of educating them on the history of the Order and its importance within the world. It is designed, according to this source, to impress and to leave initiates awestruck rather than to terrify and intimidate them. The ceremony as depicted by Rosenbaum seemed too much like a schlocky, horror, B movie to be real. One Bonesman who attended Yale during the 1970s says that the process is more concerned with passing on the Order's history than with cheap scares. As such, it has been suggested that Rosenbaum witnessed something else. Perhaps a skit or prank organized by the group in the knowledge that he was watching. It might have been a joke which blew out of proportion or a deliberate sleight of hand designed to distract from the Order's real rituals. By giving the public a theatrical, almost comedic image, the Order was able to present themselves as silly and non-threatening. While Rosenbaum might have gained the Order more attention, it was publicity that was manageable and dismissible. Indeed, one Bonesman, when asked about the subject, admitted that they purposefully wanted to joke around with the journalist and were well aware of his recording.

Recruitment

Getting a grip on the society's most secret rituals, it seems, is very difficult. There is a determination to keep the most intimate of the group's secrets secret, and they are willing to misdirect, distract, and otherwise obstruct in order to maintain this veil of mystery. Accordingly, you would imagine that this makes recruitment into the Order a very tricky business. One wrong move and the Bonesmen might find themselves exposed by someone who is willing to trade all of their secrets for some quick cash or notoriety. So how are candidates selected?

The process of recruitment for the Order is known, as we have already mentioned, as "tapping." During the early years of the society, this was a very private affair. On the designated evening, the fifteen extant Bonesmen would meet together in the darkest of the night and move silently around campus. When arriving at the residence of their intended recruit, they would enter baring a real skull and bones. Presenting the remains to the target, they would ask the recruit whether they accepted the society's invitation. Regardless of the response, the group would then file out in total silence. Only later would the recruit know their fate.

But this process soon became notorious on the Yale campus. After a short while, the other students realized what would be happening and became understandably fascinated by the tapping of the new members. Rather than a group of fifteen cloaked figures, there was soon a procession of interested parties who followed the Bonesmen around campus. This meant that they were forced to abandon their proclivity for meeting at midnight, and in order to maintain some semblance of mystery, began to appear to new recruits at more random hours. The group was whittled down until it was just one or two senior Bonesmen (people who understood the gravitas and the importance of the invitation), who arrived at the younger man's dorm and presented their offer. On the rare occasions when the student declined the offer of the Order, increasingly senior members of the society would be sent to repeat the invitation in a more persuading manner.

Tapping as a Competition

At the end of the 19th Century, however, the sheer number of societies on the Yale campus and their similar recruitment policies meant that the tapping of new recruits became a big event. For most societies, there was an "A-list" of desirable recruits and then a backup list should they be rejected. For Skull and Bones, however, the possibility that they might be rejected was nonsensical. For a long time, there was resistance to the idea that they might be in any way rejected by potential recruits, who would surely be mad not to join. However, the increased competition for the new waves of Yale scholars meant that by 1928, the society had received eight rejections from those that tapped. Unlike the other societies, they refused to do any preliminary investigations into who might accept and who might decline their offer. From then on, they were more organized and more determined to land their first choices when it came to filling out the Tomb with the best and the brightest.

Accordingly, there is a history within the society of attempting to hoodwink the other groups in order to land the most desirable targets. In 1871, another group named Scroll and Key attempted to organize the societies on campus to move the initiation ceremonies forward in the calendar in order to better teach the incoming students coming into the club before the older members graduated. Skull and Bones declined to answer the letter, and it was assumed that the tapping would occur at the regular time. Instead, Skull and Bones launched their recruitment a full three weeks before the other societies. The move was brash enough to make the local news, while the Yale Literary Magazine (whose editor was a Bonesman) took a gloating approach to the reportage.

A similar event occurred in 1917. Provoked by the onset of the World War I and the American involvement in the conflict, the three most important societies on campus decided to begin their recruitment early. A pair of Bonesmen, Robert Lovett and F. Trubee Davison, had been instrumental in setting up a Naval Aviation Unit made of Yale students in preparation for the war. Davison's father was the financier for the project. Such was the wealth poured into the unit that they earned the nickname "the millionaires' unit." As the move to war escalated and other societies suggested that recruitment begin early, Skull and Bones found that they had been distracted and demanded that the recruitment be delayed in order to allow them to catch up. The date they demanded was the 19th of April, almost two full weeks after America had decided to enter into the war. During this time, the Naval Aviation Unit had partnered fully with the military and had been flown out to West Palm Beach to begin full preparations. With them went a huge number of the most desirable candidates for the recruitment that yea. They stayed together in an old hotel. This was where the recruitment ceremony took place, with the other groups having to enter into the organization of the Skull and Bones in order to try and get their men. The choices were made at the base, information which was then relayed through telephone and telegram conversations back to campus. Arriving at the base, former Bonesmen who were in the area were able to initiate the new members before the other societies realized what was happening. Thanks to their process of taking the group away from the campus and being prepared for the initiation right away, they had secured their desired candidates.

A Public Affair

Up until the end of the 20th Century, the names and details of those who had been selected by the Yale societies would be printed in the Yale Daily News and the New York Times. With column space limited, the names printed were only those selected by the most important societies, while others could have their names printed in exchange for a small fee. In 1919, following that year's tapping, the Yale Daily News changed the process. In the place where one might expect to see the list of all the top societies, there was instead only the details for the very first and the very last man to have been tapped by Skull and Bones, written in large print. This kind of exclusivity was unprecedented. It should be no surprise to see that the managing editor of the publication was a member of the Order, Henry Luce. Luce would play a key role in founding Time Inc. by the next issue and issued an apology for the "oversight." But his actions confirmed to many what was already known to most on campus. While there were a number of secret societies on the Yale campus, there was only really one with any real influence and only one that really mattered: the Order of the Skull and Bones.

One leaked document from the 1960s possibly best represents the approach of the Order to recruiting new members. The guide on how to approach potential new members is very strict. It impresses upon the Bonesmen that they should under no circumstances appear to be desperate to recruit a certain member. They must instead always remain "cool and concise," with the privacy of the Order prioritized above all else. Trying too hard to convince a potential member seems out of sorts and, in so powerful a society, not an impression they need to make. Instead, an offer is extended, and should it be met with any reticence, the recruit should be informed about the nature of the society and the advantages it will bring. The Order of the Skull and Bones is "based on such intangible factors that we cannot meaningfully convey to you either its nature or its quality." Join the Order, it suggests, and you will be welcomed into an inner circle and provided with riches and knowledge beyond your wildest dreams. Since the middle of the 20th Century, the tapping of Yale students had again become a private matter.

Recruiting Traditions

Recruitment for the Order follows a precedent. Each year, there is a willingness to offer membership to the same "types" of student, those who fit into a mold of what has come before. This process has led to other societies accusing the Order of recruiting "tokens," students taken for their profile rather than their merit. But the history of who might be recruited is limited the further back we look into Yale's history. For example, there was a long period of time when the large majority of students fit into one particular demographic: white, protestant Americans from a privileged background. It was many years before Catholic or Jewish students made up a sizable portion of the student body, longer still before non-white or female students were allowed to attend the university. Ideally, each current member looks through the incoming possibilities and selects the person that will replace them. These choices are then presented before the Order, who can approve or veto their inclusion. One veto (otherwise known as a blackball) and the candidate might be asked to appear before the society and present their case. Two vetoes and the candidate is automatically rejected.

Though many of the early years of Skull and Bones were filled with the same type of person, later years have seen the remit expand. A leaked document from 1968 outlines the "ideal" group who might be recruited in any one year. Based almost entirely on stereotypes, the literature suggests the following be recruited:

1. The captain of the football team
2. The chairman of the Yale Daily News
3. Someone who is a "conspicuous radical"
4. A Whiffenpoof (an acapella singer)
5. The captain of the swim team
6. A "notorious drunk" who has an average of 94
7. A filmmaker
8. Someone known for their political columns
9. The leader of a religious group
10. The chairman of the Lit
11. A foreign person
12. A "ladies man" who possesses two motorcycles

13. A former service man
14. A "negro" providing there are "enough to go around"
15. Someone whom no one in the group had heard of, "ever"

There is no doubt that the precedents have changed and altered over the years, moving in flux with the changing patterns of the Yale student body and the political and social movements of the day. There is, however, a seeming desire to recruit both the best members (those with a high profile around campus) and a need to keep the group balanced. There are accommodations made for those who have had family in the organization before and a willingness to alter the patterns in years when suitable candidates might not present themselves. As we have not been able to look upon a similar list from recent years, we do not yet known how the recruitment criteria have changed in the last decades. However, this list of fifteen stereotypes informs us of the process of tapping and how it might follow a predetermined route, rather than the whims of the current members. Here, we can see the precedents and the importance placed on both history and secrecy.

The Initiation Ceremony

So, now that we know just how much interest there is in what happens during the initiation of the Skull and Bones members and the extent to which they recruit the ideal members, what do we really know about the rituals and ceremonies that take place within the Tomb? The problem here is that many of the most important processes remain hidden and secret. The truth about the Skull and Bones is that the real power resides among those who have already graduated from the university, rather than those who are currently in attendance. The Order is a bond shared by Presidents, CEOs, media bosses, and many others. Through the Russell Trust Association, they own and operate the apparatus that is used to recruit the next generation of influential people. Once in the crosshairs of the Order, they are bonded together while at Yale. But in order to mark them out as potential powerbrokers of the future, they must be inducted into the Order in the correct manner. Of all the rituals that are said to happen behind closed doors, the initiation ceremony is perhaps the one about which we have the greatest amount of knowledge. Even then, it is difficult to separate verifiable fact from supposition-based fiction. If we want to learn more about the initiation ceremony, we must trust the former Bonesmen who have revealed information to the world.

The trouble with this is that they typically refuse to give their real names. While they might divulge their identity to the journalists and authors writing pieces about the Order, these names are very rarely made public. In biographies and confessional pieces by confirmed Bonesmen, many choose to remain decidedly silent about what happens within the society. So we must turn to the anonymous sources and try and piece together bits of information and use separate accounts to corroborate one another. In this regard, there is an element of trust that must be exercised. Like Rosenbaum before us, there is the pratfall awaiting anyone curious about the Skull and Bones. But there is at least a vague comprehension of the information that we believe we can verify. If you are curious about the initiation ceremony of the Order of the Skull and Bones, the process by which some of the world's most powerful people are inducted into a secret society, then read on.

According to Lanny Davies, the initiation into the Skull and Bones was "the most harrowing" of all such ceremonies. In a review of the lore as established in the 1960s, Davies described how an initiate must face a combination of current and former members. The neophyte is alone, without friends or support. Davies's account suggests that a physical beating took place, after which the recruit was stripped naked and forced to wrestle with Bonesmen. The next part of the ceremony is one of the biggest rumors that concerns the Skull and Bones. According to these rumors – and recounted by Davies – the initiate must then lay down inside an empty coffin. Still naked, they are commanded to begin masturbating and must speak aloud their sexual history for all of the Order to hear. This type of behavior is typical for many secret societies and cults, who conduct such rituals in order to bond the recruit to the Order for as long as possible. Should they later decide to leave, this detailed sexual history added to the rumors of "deviant" rituals is thought to be enough to destroy any credibility that a person might have. Certainly, reports in Observer Life magazine during the Presidency of George W. Bush posit the idea that he might have taken place in such a practice. Examples of such behaviors can be seen in the rumored activities of Scientology, a religion that encourages new members to confess their sins and then uses this information to influence the person's future decisions. It is a means of giving up control and freedom to the group in exchange for greater power or truth. But whether it is something that takes place today is another matter. There seems little doubt among scholars of the Order of the Skull and Bones that teenage sexual braggadocio might have been common in the early days of the Order, especially mixed with the hazing one might normally expect from college societies. The adolescent nature of the recruits and current members adds weight to this, though many have sought to dispel rumors that the modern initiation is anything like what is described by Davies.

A More Modern Ceremony

Instead, the supposed modern version of the initiation ceremony is likened more to a theatre performance. One member who now works as an engineer described it as being like something from Harry Potter book. Described variously by the same witness as "goofy" and "exciting," or intentionally scary and worrying, the effect seems to depend on the student in question. Some take it more seriously than others, while a great deal of the effectiveness of the ceremony likely comes down to which Bonesmen perform the ritual and how much conviction they are able to implement in their role. There is typically a consistency relating to things like costumes, props, and the words that are used, though each generation of Bonesmen put their own spin on the ceremony itself.

Before the ceremony takes place, the Order must ensure that they have the right tools to do the job. This means that they will need to collect the following:

- Black ribbon
- Black sealing wax
- Black ink
- Reams of red paper
- Pins for the new members
- The Black Book (in which the overseer records notes about the ceremony)
- A scrapbook for the new members

The person placed in charge of the ceremony takes on the traditional title of Uncle Toby, the name given to every Bonesman who conducts the initiation ceremony on any given year. Before the ritual itself takes place, the Uncle Toby and his fellow members (plus any returning members) will rehearse the ritual and plan for the coming ceremony. Before the ritual begins, the members of the Order will venture out onto campus and travel to the confirmed recruits' residences. Typically on a Sunday evening, this visit will involve the delivering of a red packet. The red packets are traditionally prepared invitations containing details of when and where to meet, as well as the Skull and Bones insignia. It will be sealed with the black wax and the seal of the Order, sometimes burned using a candle. The initiation ceremony will be arranged for a short time later. Before this time, four Bonesmen will pay a visit to the new member and provide him with a formal invitation.

The delivery of the formal invitation is a ceremony within itself. Four Bonesmen will arrive at the home of the recruit. One, a guard, will check to see whether the nearest bathroom is empty. When it is, he will signal to the speaker among the group. One of the two so-called "shakers" will knock "soundly" on the recruit's door. Once the person within is correctly identified, he is grabbed by the shakers and dragged into the bathroom. The guard will shut the door behind them and ensure that no one else is able to enter. As the recruit is led into the room and forced to stand facing a corner, the speaker will announce when and where he must travel to take part in the initiation ceremony. He is told to wear no metal, Sulphur, or glass, and to knock three times upon the door of the Tomb. The recruit must remember these instructions but keep quiet. A white packet is then thrown at his feet, thought to contain a formal invitation, while the Bonesmen exit. Throughout, the recruit must stare into the wall in the corner.

Once the recruit is suitably informed, then the process of preparing the Tomb for the ritual begins under the guidance of the anointed Uncle Toby. We know that the ritual itself has changed since the early days of the Order, when the new member was dragged before "the Devil" and then struck with the flat of a sword in a twisted parallel of the tradition of knighthood. This is where the name "Knights of the Order of the Skull and Bones" derives. Before there was an official residence for the society, the ritual took place in the Sheffield Scientific School, the office of Benjamin Silliman (one of the first Order members). The modern version of the initiation differs, however, in that it has taken a more theatrical approach.

The Initiation Night

On the night when the ceremony is set to take place, as many Bonesmen as possible are gathered together. This is not only those who are currently in the Order, but also alumni who travel back to campus. Traditionally, there are at least eleven graduated members who are contacted up to a month before the evening in question. Many of the more famous members are reached out to, with the idea being to impress the new recruits and show a raw demonstration of the influence and power the groups wields. During the evening, the new recruits will be lead through every room in the Tomb, but the ritual itself will always take place in the Inner Temple. By the time the actual ceremony takes place, those involved will have rehearsed their actions to the point where they can be conducted without error. All furniture is removed from the Inner Temple, clearing space enough for all of the members apart from a number of chairs.

When a new recruit approaches the door and attempts to knock as they have been told, they will discover that the door opens before them. As soon as they step inside, a Bonesman will appear out of the darkness and thrust a hood over the unsuspecting head. The first port of call is the Firefly Room, one of the many living quarters within the building. Here, the hood is removed, only for the recruit to find themselves in the pitch-black darkness. The only things visible are the Bonesmen's lit cigarettes that float around the room, leading to the Firefly nickname. The neophyte is pushed into a chair and receives instructions. Before they can really get a grip on what else is in the room, the hood is thrown back over their head. This is when the recruit is marched from room to room, during which time they are subjected to torrents of abuse and insults from the hordes of Bonesmen who have gathered in the Tomb. Throughout, strands of the Order's history are woven into the tour, and the recruit learns about the importance of certain rooms. During this time, his hand is run along a piece of wood, which he is told is a coffin. He is made to listen to the sounds of running water, which gave birth to the idea that there might be a swimming pool in the depths of the property. Instead, the sounds are effected by the Bonesmen to confuse and disorientate the neophyte.

Inside the Inner Temple are two chairs and a table. The Bonesmen, wearing masks, move into the room in their robes. The designated Uncle Toby has a special set of robes, while the person who is set to play the role of the Little Devil also has a distinctive outfit, resembling Satan himself. The Little Devil hides in the room, waiting. A Bonesmen with the deepest voice is selected to read and is made to dress in a Don Quixote style. One current Bonesman dresses as the Pope, taking a seat to the left of the fireplace, and perches his foot on skull carved from stone. Four of the Bonesmen are designated as shakers, usually the largest among the Order, while one person is dressed as Elihu Yale, one of the school's most important benefactors. The figure is made to sit in another chair, holding open a Greek book fixed with an upside-down pin representing the Skull and Bones. The others are there to provide a deafening noise, a disorientating sound made of clattering metals and drums. Those who have specific costumes are symbolically important, while the remainder of the group add to the atmosphere. No one in the room is identifiable as all are masked.

Once the stage is suitably set, it is time to retrieve the oath of secrecy from its resting place. Kept in a draw in the table that stays in the room, it is removed and placed on the top of the table. Next to the oath is a skull fashioned into a drinking vessel and named Yorrick after the play Hamlet. This skull is filled with a dark red liquid chosen to represent blood (though it is rarely the real thing.) This skull is then taken and placed at the foot of the Madame, before Uncle Toby announces the name of the next neophyte to join the order. As the name is announced, the masked men begin to make as much noise as possible, until the atmosphere is deafening as the hooded figure is led into the room. Soon, everyone is screaming the name of the new recruit. Shoving the neophyte to the center of the Inner Temple, his hood is ripped away just as the noise reaches a crescendo. The shakers begin to drag the recruit towards the oath on the table, and soon the chants change to "read, read, read!" From this point onwards, after reading the oath, the neophyte is bound to secrecy.

The neophyte is then grabbed by the shakers and dragged before a portrait of the goddess Eulogia. There is just enough time to look at the picture before they are again grabbed and dragged back to the table. Again, the chants sound up, demanding that they read the oath of secrecy. Once this is done, they're taken back to another picture, before returning to the table, returning to a different picture, and so on. Each time the neophyte is placed before a new picture, the Bonesmen chant the name of the subject. Finally, the recruit is shoved down before Uncle Toby, and the room falls quiet. The robed figure reads out his full name – Uncle Toby Philamagee Phimalarlico Carnicks Carnickesi Carnickso McPherson O'Phanel – and the crowd then demands that the neophyte repeat the name back. When he cannot, there is a calamitous din, and the shakers drag the recruit away and throw him down before a picture of Judas Iscariot. The crowd chants Judas's name three times before the recruit is dragged to the feet of the Madame. Here, he must drink the 'blood' from the skull. As he does so, the Little Devil springs from his hiding place and begins to whip the recruit. The shakers once more take hold of the new member and march him to the feet of the Pope, while the Little Devil continues to whip him. The recruit must kiss the Pope's slipper, which is perched atop the stone skull. Once this is done, the neophyte moves from the Pope to Don Quixote, standing in front of the fireplace with a sword clasped in his right hand. The crowd falls silent again as the neophyte drops to his knees. Don Quixote reaches out with the sword, taps the kneeling recruit on the left shoulder, and names him as a Knight of Eulogia. Elsewhere in the room, the Tocsin is rung three times. Around the Inner Temple, all the Bonesmen take up chants of "Bones!" repeating the word over and over. As their shouts get louder, the neophyte is grabbed and taken before Elihu Yale and told to read the book open on his lap. When it becomes clear that the recruit – in the dark and astonished by the ritual – cannot read, then the crowd chants to admonish him. The shakers enter once more, pick the neophyte up, and walk him to the door of the room. From here, they are thrown into the waiting crowd who hustle and jab at the recruit. The initiation ritual, at last, is complete.

This is repeated fifteen times exactly. The only difference in the practice is the role of the recruit who is dubbed as the new Little Devil. Of all the recruits, the extant members will select one of them to take on the title. The Order's bylaws dictate that the new Little Devil's feet must never touch the ground of the Inner Temple. Accordingly, the recruit is turned upside down by the shakers and must journey through the ritual while turned the wrong way. This includes the drinking of the blood from the skull and the kissing of the Pope's foot, which must be done upside down. According to those who have passed through the ritual, it can be equal parts exhilarating and frightening. The sensory shock of the sound, the light, and the commands can remove the weight of any expectations one might have about the Order. Until one has travelled through the ceremony and been welcomed into the society, it's probably impossible to understand exactly how the ritual feels and how it might seem to any budding new recruit.

Minor Rituals

Following this ritual, there are a number of smaller ceremonies relevant to a number of the rooms within the Tomb. One of the more important events is the time at which all of the recruits are sat down and the Patriarchs inform them about the history and the importance of the Order. This takes place in the dining room, where lessons on lore and rules are dished out. The following party lasts all of the night, welcoming the newest members of the Skull and Bones into the fold. At this point, each of the recruits is awarded their golden Skull and Bones pin, is told how the locks to the building function, is made to meet the staff of the building and the stewards, and is allowed to share in the literature specific to the Order including the Bones Bible. By this point, the guide to the rituals of the Order declares that the recruits are now officially the "new keepers of the secrets of Skull and Bones."

There are a great many rumors about the ceremonies of the Order of the Skull and Bones. There is no doubt that there are certain rituals that have not yet become public knowledge. There is a willingness from many people to believe almost all of the stories that are told about the initiation ceremony. However, the initiation ritual is hardly the crux of the Order's power. Instead, it is the entrance point for the real power that comes much later. As we will see later in the book, the members of the Order wield a disproportionate amount of power. After recruits have been sealed into the membership of the Order, they become bonded to the society for life. It engenders them with the connections and social links that can make real changes in the world. Even for those who are from a less privileged background than the rest can expect to benefit from the advantages that the membership of the Skull and Bones brings. Not every member of the Order has gone on to achieve astonishing wealth, though a huge number of America's wealthiest families have had some contact with the Order at one point or another. There is a great fascination with the rituals of the Skull and Bones because ceremonies such as the initiation enter many people into a shared group that has members in every strata of society. Though it might seem strange and even silly at points, rituals such as these seemingly demonstrate the depth of the bond that is shared by the men and women of Skull and Bones.

While traditional views of secret societies would involve authentic demon worship and traces of the truly occult and strange, the modern view of the Order is that these ceremonies are simply a starting point. Rather, their real power lies elsewhere.

The Network of the Bonesmen

It is hard to impress upon people the importance of the Order of the Skull and Bones without mentioning to them the people who have made up the membership lists of one of the United States' oldest secret societies. In this chapter, we will work through a number of the better known members of the Order and place them in a context which demonstrates their power, influence and importance. But in addition to those who are listed below, there should follow an assurance that there is always a huge number of people whose names do not make the lists. These people have been influential in their own special ways, often facilitating and helping those who are in real power. They are often lawyers, doctors, researchers, and CEOs. Those whose names might not be the most eye catching, but whose work is equally felt by the rest of society.

The discussion below is not presented in any order, but it can help to think about the legacy of the Order as a complex interweaving spider's web of power and contacts. Similarly, there will be an emphasis placed on the relationship shared between the order and the specific individuals, rather than a list of that respective individual's accomplishments. For more information on the people listed below, a wealth of information is available on the Internet. Accordingly, rather than separate the members out into separate sections, the chapter will attempt to illustrate their connections and the ways in which the Order intersects on the lives of many people all at once.

The Bush Legacy

Perhaps the greatest interest in the Order of the Skull and Bones can be traced back to one family. While they were not involved in the creation of the society, the Bush family have been one of the most powerful families in America over the past half-century. Two generations have held the office of the President of the United States, and other members of the family have worked on many layers of the political world for decades now. As well as this, two of the most prominent members of the family, George H. W. Bush and George W. Bush (his son), are confirmed Bonesmen. Throughout their careers, their political allies, their business partners, and their rivals have all held an association with the Order. As such, the modern Bush family makes an excellent lens through which the entirety of the modern network of Bonesmen can be examined.

The first political campaign of George W. Bush took place in 1978. While running for Congress, Bush garnered a great deal of publicity about his father's involvement in the CIA, the Trilateral Commission, and both generations' involvement in Skull and Bones. An incident is described in a biography of the future president in which Mel Turner, a radio host, hosted an afternoon debate about the topic. Turner was right to the point, voicing concerns (supposedly shared by many other Texans) that the young George was somehow a tool of a shadowy government cabal. Turner went as far as to dub the politician a "tool of the eastern kingmakers." Bush, tired of being lambasted for his paternal and social connections, was adamant that there was no one out there who held the power to change his mind on any matter. After the interview was over, Bush refused to shake Turner's hand and labelled him an "asshole."

But the accusations didn't end there. Kent Hance, a Democrat, accused Bush of riding along on his "daddy's coattails," following on from accusations of elitism. Hance was decisively victorious in the election, but it was the accusations of shadowy support that followed Bush around for decades. So much so, in fact, that George W. Bush chose to address such charges in his autobiography, labelling the accusations so random and disparate that they were "virtually impossible to refute." It was not the first time that someone from the Bush family had exhibited annoyance at these kind of rumors, as both his father and grandfather and faced similar issues. In 1966, for example, his grandfather Senator Prescott Bush had been forced to deal with the suggestion that the Senate might have been under the control of what was called an "establishment" group. According to some reports, George H. W. Bush saw his glittering Curriculum Vitae (and its inclusion of Skull and Bones) as a hindrance, causing accusations and conspiracies to follow him from job to job.

It should come as no surprise, then, to see that George W. Bush went to such lengths to distance himself from the "establishment." In fact, there is a gap of twenty years between the times when George graduated Yale and returned to the campus. He has discussed the "intellectual snobbery" that he feels surrounds the place and has described Yale as epitomizing the kind of "East Coast attitude" that he resents. When he returned again to the campus in 2001, he took the opportunity to make jokes about the school, where he was a not-particularly exceptional student. For some people, however, these constant throwbacks to his alma mater are nothing but an attempt to distance George W. Bush from the home of the Order of the Skull and Bones.

Networking

It is undeniable that one of the chief benefits of joining the organization is the networking opportunities that it presents. It brings together different types of people, as well as those who are used to wielding power. At any given time, with the induction of fifteen new members each year, there are roughly 800 living Bonesmen. For so many of them to be occupying positions of power demonstrates the advantage that this networking opportunity provides. Since its inception every President who spent time at Yale as an undergraduate was a member of the Order. In 2004, the Presidential election pitted George W. Bush against John Kerry, another Bonesman. Though Bush won, the influence of Skull and Bones on American politics was never clearer.

But it's not just the political sphere that's felt such a big influence from Skull and Bones. One of the most obvious ways in which the Order has infiltrated a power structure is in the academic structure of Yale University. It was only until very recently that the authorities on campus were not dominated by former Bonesmen. With people in high ranking parts of the Yale infrastructure, Skull and Bones could do a lot to offer protection for their members. For example, two students faced expulsion in 1873 for below-standard results in their exams. One of the two was a member of the Order, and one was not. The Bonesman was allowed to continue his studies and retook his exam six weeks later. The other student faced a term of suspension and was restricted from retaking any exams until the following term. According to one professor (and Skull and Bones alumni), the reasoning was that this was a "special case." Such an event led the Yale magazine the Iconoclast to publish their views that Skull and Bones was the "bane" of Yale University.

Similarly, in the 1920s, the disciplining of any students at the university came under the purview of a student council. In 1928, three quarters of the council (including its chairman) were members of Skull and Bones. When a case came before them that suggested that one of their fellow society members might have been caught cheating on his exams, they were the ones who were able to determine the suitable punishment. They chose to do nothing. This decision angered the other members of the class to the extent that they formally complained to the council and demanded an answer. The students were told that, in this case, the council simply preferred not to have to make a decision. Just a year later, the student council was abandoned. With so many important people in such high ranking places of the Yale institution, Skull and Bones were able to protect their members from some of the worst punishments offered up by the university. Already, before even graduating, members were able to take advantage of the institutional privilege exercised by the Order of the Skull and Bones.

Family Histories

We have already examined the ideal selection criteria that the Order will examine when making its decisions on who to join. But just as with the manner in which the Order is capable of influencing the wider world, there have been accusations of nepotism in the recruitment of certain people. Being a family member of a noted Yale student or former Bonesman is an excellent way in which you can advance your cause for being selected. This, perhaps, is the chief reason why George W. Bush was selected. A self-confessed "C student," he was hardly the stand-out academic candidate in his class. However, both his father and grandfather had been prominent Bonesmen, Yale graduates, and politicians. It was almost predetermined that young George would be joining the society.

Prescott Bush, George W. Bush's father, benefitted hugely from his connections to the Order. At the age of thirty-one, after graduating Yale as a Bonesman, he was invited to join W. A. Harriman & Company. Owned and operated by two Bonesmen and the father of a Bonesman, the investment bank was the largest private banking institution in the United States. Prescott didn't have a huge CV, having worked for another Bonesman – Wallace Simmons – for a short while. But Prescott was one of the most active Skull and Bones alumni and often returned to the Tomb. The networking opportunities it offered were unsurpassed and allowed him to waltz into a high-paying banking position that would lay the foundation for his wealth and political power.

The man who had started the company that employed Prescott, Averell Harriman, was also a Bonesman and was awarded with a number of incredibly important positions. As well as having his name above the door on America's biggest private bank, he was later elected as the Governor of New York before taking a position as the ambassador to the USSR during the height of World War II. Speaking years later about what the Order did for him, Harriman said that it gave him purpose. Just like Prescott Bush, he took the society very seriously and was seen to venture back to the Tomb on a number of occasions. There were suggestions that he would discuss vital national security secrets over his regular dinners at the Skull and Bones Temple, but that he would never, under any circumstances, discuss the activities of the Order with anyone but a member. He took the code of secrecy incredibly seriously. Indeed, when Harriman was moving his codified dispatches between London and Moscow during the war, he was allowed to select the combination to his diplomatic case. He chose the number 322.

Nor was Averell Harriman the first of his family to take advantage of the Skull and Bones networking opportunity. A man named Stuyvesant Fish (a Bonesman from 1905) gave Averell's father his first big job in the railroad industry. Edward Harriman, Averell's father, had attended Yale in the class preceding Fish and had been in the Order when Fish arrived. By the time of his death, it is estimated that his estate was worth some $100 million, largely built up from railroad interests. In 1904, Edward Harriman tried to influence the politics of the country, promising that he would raise campaigning money for Teddy Roosevelt on the condition that Roosevelt appoint Chauncey Depew as the ambassador to France. Depew was not only a Senator, but he was also a fellow Bonesman and a friend of the railway industry. Harriman raised the money as promised, but when Roosevelt won, he discovered that the President was going to renege on the deal. To try and reconcile things between himself and the President, Harriman dispatched an intermediary, naturally a Bonesman, named Maxwell Evarts. At all times, those Harriman elevated and trusted the most were the people who shared their membership in a secret society from the Yale campus.

Even the formation of W. A. Harriman and Company was made possible through the connections gardened at the Order of the Skull and Bones. The firm was founded thanks to financial backing from Percy Rockefeller, a Bonesman in 1900 and part of one of the richest American families of all time. Added to this one bank, Averell Harriman was able to convince Percy to invest in a number of other ventures, such as a burgeoning aerospace business that belonged to Averell's brother-in-law. When seeking out good employees, the Harriman family often turned to Yale graduates and showed particular favor to those who had been in the Order. All across the country, many large and powerful firms were being run in exactly the same manner. The connections that one made while a member of the Yale Skull and Bones society could provide lasting employment at the very top of the American business pyramid. Often, Bonesmen would specifically seek out and trust one another when populating their companies with employees. Slowly, many of America's most important institutions – politics, universities, and business – became another networking opportunity for the Order of the Skull and Bones. And it is a legacy that has continued to this day. The modern iterations of Harriman's bank – Brown Brothers Harriman and Company – had nine of their twenty-six partners as alumni of the Order as recently as 1972, while the chairman himself – Frederick Allen – was a member in 1900.

Pre-University Days

Even before arriving at Yale, it is possible for Skull and Bones to have an influence over a person's life, especially for those who have previously had family members in the Order. Taking the Bush family again as an example, it's possible to see the connections to the Order affecting a person's life. There is a story from the military days of George H. W. Bush, who was serving in the Pacific during the World War II. It was the 2nd of September, 1944, and George was the lieutenant of a flight crew who had just received orders to destroy a radio installation located in Chichi-jima. Before they set off, George was approached by a man who had been in the Order two years previously. Knowing that George had ties to Skull and Bones, he plead to be taken along on the mission despite his lack of experience. Ted

White, as he was known, was a gunnery officer and replaced his equivalent Leo Nadeau during the mission after getting approval from Bush and his commanding officer. The mission went wrong, however, with the Japanese shooting down the plane. Bush, managing to send the explosion payload before ejecting, was dismayed to learn that Ted White had been killed in the mission.

It was three years later when George H. W. Bush was telling the story to a captive room. Inside the Tomb, George told his new society mates about how he had encountered a Bonesman before and how it had ended in tragedy. According to reports from the night, Bush was regretful that he ever "let him go" and wished he hadn't allowed White along on the mission. To those in the room that night, it seemed as though there was a sense of real anguish in the new recruit's face. It was that year that George, as the son of Prescott Bush, was receiving the honor of being the last (and most important) tap. Having already been deeply affected by the death of a fellow Bonesman, Bush was now on the inside and ready to start fostering the relationships that would suit him so well later in life. It wouldn't be long before his connections within the Order were cemented. Alexander Ellis would go on to become an insurance executive and would be the roommate of John H. Chafee, a future senator. Ellis would marry Nancy, George's sister. Along with James L. Buckley (another future senator), George and Chafee would be the ushers at the wedding.

In fact, George H. W. Bush's life just after graduation can give a fantastic insight into the extent to which Skull and Bones connections can facilitate success and power within those who join. Straight after leaving Yale, Prescott Bush was prepared to break the rule against nepotism that had been implemented in the Brown Brothers Harriman bank and wanted to offer his son a job. George turned them down, however, as well as refusing a job with his uncle, George Herbert Walker (a Bonesman in 1927). On the suggestion of his father, he turned to another former Order member, Neil Mallon, who had been placed as the president of Dresser Industries by Roland Harriman at the suggestion of Prescott. The company worked with oil in the Southwest of the United States, and George was hired as the only trainee that year, supposedly on the promise that he'd have the chance to run the company someday. Bush spent years under the tutelage of Mallon, to the point where he would eventually name a son, Neil, after his mentor. Even for a Yale graduate, the chances laid out in front of George H. W. Bush when he left university offered him untold fortune and power. He could have worked in finance, investment banking, or a multitude of other industries – essentially, anywhere the Bonesmen held influence. Being able to turn so many excellent opportunities down demonstrates the capabilities of the Order of the Skull and Bones when it comes to putting people in positions of power. If you possess the right connections, then it is possible to get an incredible head start in some of the country's most powerful industries. When it came time for George to start his own oil business, it was former members he turned to in order to raise the requisite funds. Even at a lower level, there were less successful Bonesmen who were encouraged to invest sums such as $40,000, enough to buy a home in 1952. From the very top down, members of the Order of the Skull and Bones were able to take care of one another.

This was particularly useful when George H. W. Bush decided to run for President. Having been in the office of Vice-President for a number of years, he had remained close to the fellow members of Skull and Bones. He held regular dinners with those from his graduation year, as well as other members of the Order who were occasionally invited. It was to these groups that Bush announced the difficulties he felt he faced as Vice-President, as well as the worries he held about running for the big office. But it was the Bonesmen who raised a great deal of money to fund his campaign. One member, William Judkins Clark, raised $400,000 all by himself, a huge amount at the time.

Loading the Deck

When he did win the Presidency, Bush held no qualms about stocking many of the best positions with former Skull and Bones men, as well as doing political favors for those who were aligned with the Order. Frederick Smith had been a member of the Order of the Skull and Bones in 1966 and had gone on to found Federal Express, one of America's biggest companies. He had headed up a group of the top 100 business people in America and had pledged their support to the Bush presidency. This favor was returned once George was in office, with FedEx receiving the highest honor that can be bestowed upon an American business, the Malcolm Bridge Quality Award (which is actually named for the son of another

Bonesman.) Of the Bonesmen Bush appointed, George H. Pfau became the director of a department named the Securities Investor Protection Corporation; Richard Anthony Moore became the Ambassador to the Republic of Ireland; and Paul Lambert (utterly lacking in any diplomacy experience) became the Ambassador to Ecuador. All of them had been members of the Order of the Skull and Bones. Furthermore, David George Ball became Assistant Secretary of Labor, Christopher Buckley became Bush's chief speechwriter, James T. Hempill joined the Department of the Interior, David Grimes became a representative of Bush during some key foreign trips, Thomas W. Mosely formed part of the delegation to Uruguay, Edward McNally wrote some of Bush's most famous speeches, and Raymond Price was awarded the job of writing Bush's speech to the Republican National Convention in 1992. Bush wasn't just giving Bonesmen posts in business and overseas, they were forming key parts of his government. Even in the CIA (where George spent time working), there were a disproportional number of Yale graduates, to the extent that members of the other agencies referred to their agents as "Yalies." Of course, among the most important assignments were those with close ties to the Order.

Listing the full extent of Skull and Bones appointments during the Bush administration would take up a huge portion of this book. Suffice it to say, Bonesmen were more than represented throughout the annals of the government, especially when you consider the fact mentioned earlier, that there were typically only 800 living Bonesmen at any one time. This is perhaps the best example of the spider web of Skull and Bones networking that we have today. Though there are further examples to be found in the world of business, media, and law, the presidency of George H. W. Bush is a fine example of the extent to which the Order of the Skull and Bones infiltrated the government. The extent to which Bonesmen were involved in the administration during this time became an open secret. It was known to most everyone who paid attention, but few dared to mention it. Perhaps this is why, by the time the Internet had risen to power and George W. Bush sought the same office, he went to great lengths to distance himself from the accusations that had trailed his father. The son has worked hard to keep himself from the accusations that have followed his father around for decades. But that ignores several salient facts. Firstly, thanks to efforts by people such as the senior George Bush, there is already in place in the government of the United States a heavy influence of those with ties to Skull and Bones. Secondly, the emergence of the World Wide Web of information – the Internet – means that it is now possible to track and trace the movements of those who are in the Order. While previously the existence of the Order was known as well as some of its members, it was difficult to disseminate this information quickly. This has not been possible, and it could be that the Order is either struggling to come to terms with this prevalence of information or (more likely) they have simply taken a greater degree of secrecy to their actions. For example, as of 2015, Austan Goolsbee has been appointed as staff director chief economist to the Economic Recovery Advisory Board started by Barack Obama, who did not attend Yale. James Emanuel Boasberg is a judge for the United States District Court for the District of Columbia. Edward S. Lampert is the chairman of Sears and Kmart. Even Academy Award nominated actor Paul Giamatti is a Bonesman. What is markedly different from the previous eras is the extent to which this information is offered much less freely. These days, one of the most famous secret societies seems to be retreating back into their more secretive past.

But despite this commitment to secrecy, the legends of the Order of the Skull and Bones have been passed down from generation to generation. It seems that, while the networking system is still in place, there is a growth in the number of theories that relate to Skull and Bones. In the next chapter, we will examine some of the most common legends, from world domination to campus pranks. Now that we have established just how real and far-reaching the network of Skull and Bones members has become, it lends credence to some of the most extreme rumors.

The Legends of the Order

Ask anyone on campus which is the strictest of all the Yale societies, and they'll give you the same answer: Skull and Bones. These rules have been misinterpreted and misconstrued over time, giving rise to some of the strangest rumors about the group. For example, an old bylaw seems to suggest that all Bonesmen must exit a room should someone utter the words "Skull and Bones" or the number "322." The legend of the rule was largely established in a novel – *Saving the Queen* by William F. Buckley – and is backed up by hearsay and whisperings, especially by those who attended the university in the 1960s. It's been a Harvard legend that all that was required to beat their academic rivals at football was to take to the field, say the name of the society, and watch half the team exit the pitch. The legend stuck so much that during the 1988 elections, a group of reporters attempted to see what George Bush would do when he heard the name of the Order. He did nothing. Some legends, it seems, are simply exaggerated, even if they do have their roots in the truth.

Strange Rumors

It seems that some of the rules and stories surrounding the legends of the Skull and Bones are now archaic. Previously, they were designed to offer some sort of protection or benefit, though they do not make as much sense in the modern world. Much like the human appendix (a carryover from earlier evolutionary times), these rules have outlived their true usefulness, though they continue to exist within each generation of Bonesmen. For example, the above rule might well have been a means of discouraging discussions about the society in the presence of non-members. Over time, the rule was misinterpreted by the public, and its purpose was altered in the minds of those who were not members. Some of the members still held to the rules and traditions out of nostalgia and respect, while others recognized rules such as this one as having outlived its purpose. A similar rule suggests that Bonesmen should not enter the Tomb in the presence of witnesses. Previous generations might have been able to look over their shoulders for human eyes, but in the modern age of electronic surveillance, this is almost impossible. Accordingly, adherence to the rule has fallen slightly by the wayside.

One rule that has continued, however, and led to the birth of many of the stranger tales of the Order, relates to the names given to members. When a person joins Skull and Bones, they are given a new name on their first day. Once this name is handed out, it will be used by the Bonesmen exclusively for the remainder of their lives. It is possible for a member to pass on a name to the new generation of recruits, a tradition that has occurred many times, and helps to bond the new Bonesmen to life within the society and within the walls of the Tomb. Certain nicknames within the group have certain connotations and are handed out accordingly. For example, the name "Magog" is given to the recruit deemed to be the most successful in their romantic endeavors, while "Gog" refers to the least successful. The tallest of the Bonesmen is named "Long Devil," while anyone who captains the Yale varsity football team is named "Boaz." "Little Devil" – the person so involved in the initiation ceremony – is the name given to the shortest member of the order. For everyone else, a name is chosen at the members own discretion. In addition, Magog and Gog are allowed to select new names should they wish.

For an example of the naming traditions in action, we should look to George W. Bush. While the world might know him by one name, Skull and Bones members know him as Temporary. According to the legends from within the Tomb, it was a name he selected on the spur of the moment and never got around to changing. If we look back a little further, rumors suggest that Temporary's father went under the title of Magog, though he was already married by the time he passed through the initiation ceremony. The title of Magog for George Bush Snr is a point of contention, however, with some Bonesmen being adamant that his nickname had been "Barebones." Whether this was hastily reworked following George's burgeoning political career or whether it's the actual name Bush selected for himself, we do not know. When looking through the archives of Skull and Bones documents that have surfaced, however, it seems that Prescott Bush was named Barebones and that this name might well have passed along the generations. However, this would lead to a question about why the junior George Bush did not inherit the title. It's a question that, like many of the Bones names, leaves the audience with nothing but further questions.

We do know the names of several of the more famous Magogs. William Howard Taft, Robert Taft (his son), and Don Schollander all bore the title. In addition, we know that F. O. Mathiessen and Amos Alonzo Stagg were both Little Devils. Details such as these hint at the reams of unknown information we have about the Order. In addition, the names themselves serve a particular function. They provide an immediate point of familiarity and discussion for Bonesmen across different generations. When requesting a favor from a fellow Bonesman, being able to use his secret name adds a touch of familiarity and trust that is not permitted to those not in the Order.

Just like the awarding of names, the title of Uncle Toby is something that is frequently misunderstood by those who are not a part of the Order. While most college societies will elect a permanent leader, Skull and Bones allows its members to take turns at assuming the role of Uncle Toby. As already discussed, the person with this title will lead the ceremonies and rituals and will also chair debates, takes notes during discussions, and typically is allowed to have the last say on anything that pertains to the society itself. This way, power is spread out among the members. Similarly, the seniors in the Order are overseen by the former members who sit on the Russell Trust Association's governing board. This board elects a President of the Society and a Treasurer, as well as the more idiosyncratic Corporal Trim (who is in charge of menus), the Secretary of the Eulogian Club (who liaises with the alumni), and the Commissary, who manages society business interests. The Secretary of the Eulogian Club sits to the right of Uncle Toby, and the Commissary sits nearest to the door. While it might seem as though the president of the society is the de facto leader or that Uncle Toby might take on that role, true power in fact resides with the Secretary of the Eulogian Club. During the 19th Century, this position had the power of veto and could approve business related to the Order. The Little Devil is equally important, as he sits to the left of Uncle Toby and is in charge of collecting any fines from members. Many of the names handed out in this manner can be traced back to the novel Tristram Shandy, where characters such as Uncle Toby and Corporal Trim feature.

These smaller rules give an example of what life might be like within the walls of the Tomb. There are other flights of fancy, such as the fact that the schedule runs on Skull and Bones Time (five minutes faster than real time), and students use their own annual calendar. But these actions typically lack far-reaching ramifications beyond the Yale campus. They might seem strange to those unfamiliar with the American academic system, but they are not entirely uncommon. However, they certainly add to the strangeness that permeates the Order. It is this uncanny appearance, coupled with the type of individuals who are involved, that gives rise to many of the theories that exist about Skull and Bones. In fact, there is an intersection between the ideas of the standard college society and the theory of a global conspiracy that can be found in the regular alumni dinners. At these events, some of the world's most powerful people are invited to rub shoulders and talk with their fellow graduates and Bonesmen. But what actually happens at these events?

Face to Face

Typically, there are two meetings a year when the alumni are invited to the Tomb. One takes place in the winter, while the other occurs close to the Yale commencement. Before each event, every living Bonesman will receive a printed invitation. Close to these dinners are the times for the official meetings of the Russell Trust Association. The more important of the two is typically regarded as the one nearest commencement, usually taking place around spring time, and the invitation to this dinner will include the list of the newest Skull and Bones members. The invitations themselves (as with all communications from the Order) arrive in black edged envelopes closed with the Skull and Bones seal. Those who cannot make it to the dinner will often provide information about their activities, in order that the society can update their records on the whereabouts of alumni. Thus far, apart from the slightly morbid aesthetics, the dinners seem like many other gatherings of university societies.

The dinners themselves are typically lavish. Including a large number of courses overseen by a number of chefs, the meal is usually followed by the smoking of cigars. In all, it seems as though the Tomb transforms into a high-class restaurant for the night. One noticeable absence, however, is alcohol. Forbidden on Skull and Bones property, the society is traditionally teetotal at all times. The rule seems designed to ensure all members remain as levelheaded as possible during their meetings, though it is said that the presence of the goddess Eulogia should be enough to act as a form of social lubricant. There have been a few exceptions, however, usually involving very fine wines. At the 1836 Christmas function, for example, two special bottles were sealed away to be enjoyed on the centenary anniversary. Despite the intent, the opening of the Tomb was seen as a special enough occasion, so they members uncorked the saved bottles several decades early and celebrated their new home in style.

Perhaps the most important part of the dinners comes at the end. While other campus societies might invite guest speakers, the only people permitted within the walls of the Tomb are Bonesmen and servants who have been bound to secrecy. As such, the only guest speakers are those who have been initiated into the Order. They discuss with those present how Skull and Bones has shaped them, helped them, and changed their lives. But the levels of secrecy that are present at these events often mean that those who are talking can do so with a degree of candor not permitted at many speaking events. McGeorge Bundy, for example, was the National Security Advisor from 1961 to 1966, serving under two Presidents. During his after-dinner speech in 1968, he took advantage of the frank and relaxed forum to speak about political figures and foreign policy without fear of his words being spread further than the Tomb. To some extent, he was right. While we know that he discussed many important subjects and discussed very privileged information with the Bonesmen, not one of them has seen fit to reveal the actual content of his conversation. This oath to secrecy on such matters is one of the bedrocks of the success of the Order, while the ability to divulge such information means that Bonesmen often have access to the very best intelligence simply by dint of association. Other speakers have included George H. W. Bush and Tex McCray, who discussed his actions during the Nixon-Khrushchev debate.

Such events are not cheap. While the attendance of the Bonesmen is free, the lavish dinners and hiring of servants is most certainly not. Add to this the upkeep and maintenance of the Skull and Bones facilities, the writing of letters and arrangements, as well as the commissioning of regular "Bones Bibles" (historical accounts of the society by members) and one is looking at a hefty price. While there are a great many members from privileged backgrounds who could undoubtedly pay their way through the Order, members are not expected to pay any dues. Instead, funding is taken from regular donations. Each year, every Bonesman receives a letter from the treasurer that requests a voluntary contribution. Such a letter might remind the Bonesman of whom they are required to pay (the Russell Trust Association) and what their last donation amounted to. While it might not seem the best means of funding, it has worked. It is thought that by the end of the 20th Century, the Order had gathered an endowment amounting to around $3million. According to the tax returns filed by the Russell Trust Association in 1997, the group's assets totaled close to $4.3million, though this shrank in the following year. Typically, the Russell Trust can expect revenues of around $750,000, with around 15% of that coming from donations. The rest can be derived from the various business interests and fundraising events held by the society.

Another key difference marking Skull and Bones out from their rival societies is the manner in which they use their wealth. Typically, societies, groups, and clubs at Yale and other universities will be known to use any money they raise to both fund themselves and to help out in the communities where they are based. This is not true for Skull and Bones. Instead, the group uses its large resources to fund its members and serve their interests "to varying degrees." In contrast, Scroll and Key – Skull and Bones' rival secret society on the Yale campus – provide a number of grants and fellowships totaling many thousands of dollars. Described by one Bonesman as being a "pretty self-serving" society, the approach is not intended to be dark or evil. Rather, it is intended to be just another way by which Skull and Bones marks itself out as different from other groups. Money from the Order rarely leaves the coffers of the Russell Trust, instead being used to pay for the upkeep and the lifestyle of the members. There is a rumor that one year, a certain unnamed Bonesman amassed a large number of drug-related debts, which he paid for by stealing a valuable rug from the organization. He sold it, and the Order used their resources to replace it. As well as this, many have suggested that there is a graduation gift given out by the society amounting to $15,000. When discussing the matter, however, one member (who graduated in 1968) mentioned that, if it were true, he was still waiting to see his gift.

While these stories have been told many times about Skull and Bones, there are a great many rumors and theories that are far more serious and move beyond simple collusion. One accusation, for example, is that Skull and Bones can be considered an anti-Semitic organization. However, there are certain flaws to this theory that has, in the age of the Internet, been commonly accepted by many. When looking closer, it seems as though the Order has counted among its number a great many members who dislike the Jewish people, though there is little to point towards the Order itself being prejudiced against them as an institution. When we look through the documented history, for example, we can uncover a letter written from Robert Nelson Corwin to Frederick Jones in 1922. The former was the Chairman of the Yale's Board of Admissions, while the latter was the Dean. Both were Bonesmen. In the letter, Corwin advocates there being a quota placed on the number of Jewish students that Yale can enroll in any given year. It contained with it an analysis of the situation concerning a seeming increase in the "students of Jewish birth," and after Jones agreed that there was such an issue, the university introduced a quota. This is backed up by the diary entries of another Bonesman, Farwell Knapp, who visited Jones later that year. In the diary, Knapp acknowledges that Jones "hates Jews," though he believes that Jones is usually impartial on such matters. Knapp discusses the efforts that have been made to reduce the number of Jewish students who hold important scholarships, and after noting that he also happens to "dislike Jews," says that he agrees with the policy. Just six months later, another diary entry suggests that the only means of dealing with the "Jewish problem" is to place trust in the actions of the Ku Klux Klan. Among those occupying high-ranking positions in the university infrastructure, many were Bonesmen and many were anti-Semites. Drawing a correlation – suggesting that it was Skull and Bones which made them thus – can be disingenuous, however, as there is little written into the actual society bylaws concerning such matters.

Crooking

Another of the more salacious rumors that circulates regarding the Order is their involvement in a number of thefts occurring around campus and beyond. Though not quite as serious as the allegations of anti-Semitism, the suggestions that Bonesmen may have stolen a number of items certainly have a great deal more credibility and these stories are accepted as truth by many people. For a long time, the moment any item of importance went missing around Yale, it was assumed that Skull and Bones will have played a part in acquiring it. The fact that non-members are prevented from entering the Tomb (a ban which includes, it is rumored, the police), the building is treated as something of a trophy cabinet for the successful heists that are conducted by the Order. These stolen items – tributes to Eulogia – have ranged from relatively minor items that are somehow connected to Yale's history to actual items of historical importance. For example, it is said that Skull and Bones have in their possession the gong which previously hung in the Treasurer's offices of the Old College, a drum from the same building, a bell taken from an East Haven church, one of the Old College's flags, and pins stolen from every single secret society that had sprung up on campus during the Order's lifetime.

The Skull of Geronimo

But there are other items that are reportedly in the possession of the Order of the Skull and Bones that would involve a far more serious accusation. One such item is the skull of Apache tribe leader Geronimo. During the 1980s, there was a concerted effort on behalf of Geronimo's modern-day descendants to find the remains of the man who went to war with the early Americans. At first, it seemed as though all of the remains had been buried in Oklahoma, inside Fort Still. Though this was the commonly accepted story of where the remains had been placed, as investigations deepened, the man tasked with finding the bones of Geronimo received a letter. Supposedly from a Bonesman, it presented the theory that the remains were not in Oklahoma, but in New Haven. Should the investigator wish to learn more, photographs could be made available. The photographs arrived and depicted both the Tomb and a glass display cabinet that contained a number of small items (stirrups, bone fragments) and – it was claimed – the skull of Geronimo himself. In addition to this, there was a written account of how it came to be in the Order's possession.

Back in 1918, a group of Bonesmen – including Prescott Bush – journeyed to Fort Still. Aware of how bad it would look should such prominent figures be caught grave robbing, they made sure to keep quiet while they dug up the remains. Two dug, two rested, and two men stood guard. Slowly, as they dug deeper, they began to uncover a saddle horn, then some rotten items of clothing, and then finally, at the very bottom of the grave, they came across the skull itself. They quickly filled the grave back in and sped back to their lodgings nearby. There, they cleaned and polished the skull. With their trophy, the Bonesmen travelled back to Yale and placed the skull of Geronimo on display.

On learning this, the investigator journeyed back to Fort Still to discern whether there was any truth to the matter. According to reports, a number of personal items had indeed been taken from the grave. The unnamed Bonesman was contacted again, and he invited the investigators to campus for a tour of the sites related to the theft. The man was clearly concerned, insisting on walking sixty feet ahead of the investigators, so as not to be associated with them. The Bonesman grew increasingly paranoid and according to the investigators, believed that people were rummaging through his garbage searching for clues. Eventually, the Bonesman vanished and went on the run.

To take matters further, the investigators and their legal team set up a meeting with Jonathan Bush, a Bonesman and brother of George H. W. Bush. The meeting took place in New York City and lasted less than an hour. Showing Bush the photographs and asking that the skull be returned in order to receive a peaceful burial, the investigators quickly realized that any genuine interest Skull and Bones had in helping them was beginning to evaporate. Though Bush promised the investigators that he would help them get what they wanted, they discovered that he was impossible to contact in the days following the meeting. It was eleven days before they could arrange another meeting. This time, Bush was accompanied by a number of other Bonesmen. They had brought with them a display case, the very same from the photographs, which contained the smaller items and the skull itself. This was given to the investigators, who remained suspicious. The skull was slightly different, though it was hard to tell why.

Taking the display case away, the investigators decided that they would need to have it analyzed. Though they found that it was actually the skull of a human, the results proved that it was actually the skull belonging to a boy aged ten years old. Added to that, it was not nearly old enough to have belonged to Geronimo. The Bonesmen tried to have the investigators sign a document that absolved them of possessing the skull. When the investigators refused and handed back the display case, they travelled back to Arizona and exercised their one remaining course of action. They asked their Senator – John McCain – to personally contact George Bush and request the return of the actual skull. After a short time, McCain responded to say that Bush would take none of his calls. To this day, the display case is kept in the Tomb. There is still a skull inside, though whether it is Geronimo's or the one belonging to the little boy, we will never know. The Bonesmen, however, still refer to the skull as Geronimo.

There is a similar story relating to the skull of Pancho Villa. A story purports that a group of Bonesmen paid a solider in the 1920s almost $25,000 to steal the skull of the Mexican leader. This is roundly denied, however, and there are reports mentioning Villa's skull inside the Tomb. Far more accurate are those that supposedly relate to the theft of the gravestone of Elihu Yale. Those who have been inside the Tomb have seen the gravestone (or an incredibly expensive, accurate replica), which is displayed alongside a note revealing that it was taken from Wrexham Church Yard. Elihu himself held a lot of ties to Wrexham, a small village in Wales, and when it was reported that the gravestone had been stolen from their churchyard, the locals requested that it be returned. The requests were ignored, and the stone remains in the Tomb to this day.

This kind of stealing is not only accepted among the Bonesmen, but it is actively encouraged. Known as "crooking," the act of stealing something from around campus or beyond is part of becoming a legitimate Bonesman. These items are then returned to the Tomb and displayed next to a small plaque which records when and who "crooked" the item. As long as there is space in the Tomb, it seems that the Bonesmen will continue to steal and pilfer.

Widespread Influence

But a far more serious claim relates to the hold Skull and Bones has over the press. For many years, the process of tapping new recruits would always include those who held the editorial positions on the student newspapers. Almost always, those in charge of the various Yale publications would have some link to Skull and Bones, which allowed them to dictate how they were presented in the press. Ever since the tail end of the 20th Century, however, this has ceased to be the case. Nowadays, the proliferation of the Internet makes it much harder to control what is published. Accordingly, very few of Yale's editors are now tapped by the Order. But their hold has always gone far beyond the campus boundaries. For example, two of America's biggest news magazines were founded by Bonesmen. Time magazine was supposedly conceived within the walls of the Tomb itself, with some saying that meetings from the 1920s will contain mentions of the magazine in the society's minutes. In addition, Today magazine was founded by Averell Harriman, merging with another publication to become Newsweek. On a number of occasions, Harriman is known to have stepped in and strong-armed the editorial team of his publications in reaction to favors and requests from fellow Bonesmen.

Other serious claims against the Bonesmen relate to their closed-door policy of admittance. We have already mentioned anti-Semitism, but for many years there was a refusal to allow the recruitment of female members. Even many decades after Yale became co-ed, Skull and Bones did not change their rules until 1991. Even today, there are alumni who regret this change in rules. It caused a great deal of consternation in 1971 when the idea was first floated. That class – now known in Skull and Bones history as the "bad club" – suggested that women might be admitted. Though the decision was accepted within the Tomb, the alumni were furious. The bad club were invited to dinner with fifty alumni as a French restaurant in New York. Some of the most prestigious members of the Order were present. It was impressed upon the group that since the alumni paid the bills of the society, they would have the final say. There was little in the way of argument, and nearly half of the bad club stormed out of the restaurant. In fact, up until

94

1991, the closest any woman could get to becoming a member would be to marry a Bonesman, in which case there was a special wedding ceremony for the happy couple. The little we know about such a ceremony comes from the sister-in-law of one Bonesman who snuck in. She reports hooded cloaks, coffins, strange incantations, and references to ghosts.

The process of accepting women was still difficult in 1991. The alumni changed the locks on the Tomb, and the Bonesmen of that year had to contact lawyers. It was finally put to a vote among the near-800 living members. It passed by a slim margin. Just before the initiation ceremonies, William F. Buckley led a group of alumni to get a court order restricting the Order's recruitment of the six woman (and nine men) who had been tapped. Another vote was held. Though it was a secret ballot, we know that John Kerry and David Boren (both Senators) voted in favor of recruiting women. Likewise, we don't know how either George Bush or his son voted, though George W. might well have revealed himself when speaking to a PBS producer many years later, confessing that he felt the group has lost its way since they began to admit women. The decision has led to a split among the alumni. Many now choose to disassociate themselves from the Order, while others are still bitter about the decision.

It has often been said that learning the secrets of the Order of the Skull and Bones can appear as something of a disappointment. For many, the inclination is to believe that it is a shadowy cabal run by the world's most powerful men. But at its heart, Skull and Bones is still very much a student society. It is run by young men (and now women) who usually hail from privileged backgrounds. At that age, they are far more likely to lean towards the typical hedonism expected of young people than the ruthless world domination thrust upon them by the many conspiracy theorists who learn about the club.

The Real Secrets?

So what are the real secrets of the Order of the Skull and Bones? In a book such as this – one which attempts to show the truth behind the rumors and deal in confirmed facts – the real secrets might never be held within the walls of the Tomb. It can help to think about the society much like an incubation chamber. At one of the country's most prestigious schools, a selection of the most privileged and brightest individuals continually recruit and bond with the next generation. In doing so, they create a structured web of power, a training ground for the networking of the elite that will help them so much in the world beyond Yale. It is true that Skull and Bones has entertained some of the most powerful people of the 19th, 20th, and 21st Centuries, but in doing so, it has provided them with a means to seize their power. The schism in the society on issues such as female admission demonstrates that there is not one single hive mind that is used to make a decision. Instead, the real power of Skull and Bones can be found in the trust it builds among members, the way in which its alumni have infiltrated the most powerful positions in the country, and the way in which it perpetuates the continuation of power being shared among the elite. Should you be a member of Skull and Bones, you will not learn the secrets of some mysterious New World Order. Instead, however, you might become a key figure in the real machinations that run the country, allowing you to glimpse and perhaps even grasp real power, all thanks to your involvement with a strange university society. The real secret of the Order of the Skull and Bones is that it is little more than smoke and mirrors. The real secret and the real power lie in what its alumni do with their connections and how it allows them to slide so seamlessly into the framework of control possessed by the United States of America.

Conclusion

There is no doubt that the Order of the Skull and Bones is one of the most important secret societies in the world. Unlike many such groups, it actually exists. Along with the Russell Trust Association, there is a real-world paper trail and physical evidence that points towards not only the society itself existing, but its membership including some of the most important people of the last two centuries. When compared to supposed societies such as the Illuminati, there is no question as to which group is more credible.

But many of the stories about Skull and Bones are seemingly just smoke and mirrors. The pagan rituals, the goddess worship, the morbid aesthetic, and the perpetual rumors that surround the society serve to distract the world from the cold, hard truth. As long as everyone believes it to be nothing more than a slightly silly, slightly archaic group, then there will be little attention paid to the fact that they have so successfully held sway over so many important industries within America.

They are a networking group, a means of picking and selecting their successors and placing them into positions of power. Skull and Bones is a proving ground for the next generation of power players, allowing the Bonesmen to evaluate and condition Yale graduates before awarding them a great deal of influence over society. It is nepotistic, reactionary, conservative, and – to the outside eye – very strange indeed. But there is no question as to whether they truly wield power. Thanks to the secretive nature of Skull and Bones, we may never know the true extent of their influence. But as we have seen behind the doors of the Tomb, we can accept that we must look further out into the real world if we are to see their real influence. The real mysteries of the Order of the Skull and Bones do not hide inside the Tomb. Instead, they are all around us.

Further reading

Benson, Michael, *Inside Secret Societies* (New York, NY: Citadel Press, 2005)

Dice, Mark, *The Illuminati* (San Diego, Calif.: The Resistance, 2009)

Goldwag, Arthur, *Cults, Conspiracies, And Secret Societies* (New York: Vintage Books, 2009)

Haag, Michael, *The Templars* (London: Profile, 2009)

Marrs, Jim, *Rule By Secrecy* (New York: Harper, 2001)

Millegan, Kris, *Fleshing Out Skull & Bones* (Walterville, OR: Trine Day, 2003)

Reynolds, John, *Secret Societies* (New York: Arcade Pub, 2011)

Sora, Steven, *Secret Societies Of America's Elite* (Rochester, Vt.: Destiny Books, 2002)

Steiger, Brad, and Sherry Hansen Steiger, *Conspiracies And Secret Societies* (Canton, MI: Visible Ink Press, 2013)

Steiger, Brad, and Sherry Hansen Steiger, *Conspiracies And Secret Societies* (Canton, MI: Visible Ink Press, 2013)

Sutton, Antony C, *America's Secret Establishment* ([Walterville, OR]: Trine Day, 2002)

Young, John K, *Sacred Sites Of The Knights Templar* (Gloucester, Mass.: Fair Winds, 2003)

More Books from Conrad Bauer

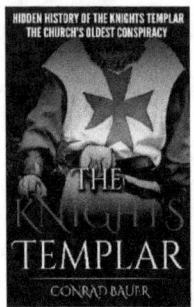

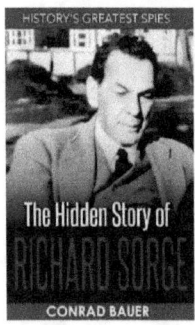

www.ingramcontent.com/pod-product-compliance
Lightning Source LLC
Chambersburg PA
CBHW072213280526
45788CB00002B/1004